"Darby Checketts has pulled off quite a feat with this mind-blowing book: he has given us a way to access the *power of opposites*, and find the huge positive energy that flows from viewing conflict as a gift. This book will free you from linear in-fighting and show you how to ride the flow of your own creativity so that you see that nothing is really wrong in your world. Powerful, and very user-friendly."

Steve Chandler
Author of *The Story of You*

"As a community college president, over the years I have been given a lot of good counsel such as: hire people unlike yourself; discuss the 'undiscussibles'; and what you resist, persists. Now, thanks to Darby Checketts, this type of wisdom and insight has been compiled into one easy-to-read book, *Positive Conflict*. The book is chock-full of delightful stories and useful tips and techniques for dealing with conflict and diversity in positive and productive ways."

Linda M. Thor, Ed.
President
Rio Salado College

"There it is in Chapter 9, the 'Navigator-Organizer-Facilitator-Visionary' matrix. I knew it. I knew I would find at least one astonishing insight that will bring me back to *Positive Conflict* time and time again when I need inspiration. The book will help you grow to appreciate the potential locked up in conflict, and learn that the gray area between dichotomous positions is actually a rainbow of opportunity."

Jody Mitchell
Executive General Manager
Spectra Energy Corporation

"In *Positive Conflict*, Darby Checketts uses accessible, yet compelling language to elevate our capacity to resolve conflict within our professional and personal circles. A rare quality of Checketts's ideas and teachings rests in their enduring relevance and applicability to a broad readership across diverse professions, personalities, ambitions, as well as spiritual and political orientations. Checketts transforms 'teamwork' from the buzzword that it has often become to a diversity-affirming, foundation principle of success."

Dr. Elavie Ndura
George Mason University

"Thought-provoking and insightful, this will become the definitive guide on how to cultivate and manage productive discussion and negotiation leading to great decision-making through *positive conflict*."

Greg Heaps
Chief Operating Officer
Allegiance, Inc.

"*Positive Conflict* has captured Darby's special way of connecting with the inner person and allowing his wisdom to seep in. He helps you see the possibilities and then teaches you how to make it happen! I have started using his recipes for leveraging conflict with amazing results! I want copies for all our leaders."

Pablo Villalon
Manager, Business Integration
Arizona Public Service

"Positively refreshing, truly and finally an authentic next step in Frederich Hegel's thesis. This book gives the reader a powerful and necessary tool kit for today's leaders to wield in a world full of conflict and challenges. The harvest will be plentiful."

Michael Del Chiaro
President
Ward/Kraft, Inc.

"Darby has done it again! *Positive Conflict* is another example of his ability to share insights and wisdom that not only have the power to transform a business, but can also transform your personal life. The book is a must-read that should be kept handy and periodically reread!"

Brenda Halpain
Controller
LifeLock

"Darby has written a refreshing and down-to-earth book on how to turn daily conflicts into positive communications both in the workplace and at home. There is no way you can read it once and get down all the things you need to do. I plan on reading it again and again."

Daniel Smith
President/CEO
Makau Corporation

"I enjoyed reading your book, Darby. Occasionally a book is written that has the potential to make an incredible difference in us all. *Positive Conflict* has that potential."

David P. Chaput
HSE Program Manager
Alaska Interstate Construction

"Again, Darby has created a book that strengthens both our family and business communication skills by providing us with principles and a framework to navigate the conflicts that are inherent between free-thinking individuals."

Michael Hawksworth
CEO/President
MSS Technologies, Inc.

"Positive Conflict gives us examples of the occasions in our lives where we fail to see the good. It teaches us how to become pro-active catalysts. As Darby talks about "polar opposites," he explains how these can not only potentially attract but also produce tremendous rewards. An incredible read!"

Roger D. Buck, CDC
Appleton Papers

"Another win-win for Darby and all that read *Positive Conflict*. Darby's ability to transform customary workplace obstacles into sensible, workable solutions is unique among authors of his ilk. He doesn't just write about *it*, he understands *it*. As a result, those of us interacting with similar issues on a day-to-day basis can actually 'see the finish line' by taking advantage of his fresh perspective and amusing anecdotes."

Marc Ruskin, ChFC, REBC, CLU, RHU
General Agent—Illinois/Wisconsin
Genworth Financial—Long Term Care Insurance Division

"Darby's book, *Positive Conflict*, is one of those rare texts that provide incisive knowledge on a topic that is applicable everywhere in life. Darby is an expert at communications in all forums; he has the unique ability to be understood by any and all audiences. I highly recommend the book."

Jeff Kimmell, RPh
Director, Distribution Strategies—
Corporate Pharmacy Management
Humana, Inc.

"*Positive Conflict* is a masterfully written how-to guide for harnessing the positive untapped power of human diversity. Darby uses vivid examples and a solid approach, which managers can use immediately to convert opposing views and ideas into action and innovation. If you lead others in work or in life, read this book. I will purchase copies for my managers and for our senior executives."

Gary J. Allen
Senior Vice President—Client Services
FPS Gold

"It never ceases to amaze me, the depth of Darby Checketts and his ability to bring complex issues such as 'conflict' to a level almost anyone can understand. *Positive Conflict* has given me a new way of looking at the issues I deal with on a daily basis."

Phillip R. Schroeder
Director, Student Financial Aid
Adams State College

"Darby Checketts's *Positive Conflict* is a must-read for managers, parents, and anyone who is uneasy about conflict in general. After reading this enlightening book, you will learn to understand conflict and welcome the good that can be generated from it. This book will forever change how I lead, manage, and communicate with my coworkers, family, and friends."

W. Patrick Snyder
Director of Human Resources
St. Mary's Food Bank Alliance

"Do you ever find yourself leaving meetings exasperated because the group cannot reach consensus? Do you work with folks who believe that getting their way is the ultimate sign of success? Do you find yourself constantly wondering why every time you are teamed with a certain person, that person just cannot see it your way? Then you need to read *Positive Conflict*. The book is about more than simply learning to get along; it's about appreciation for your fellow men—their insights and contributions—and it is ultimately about respect."

Bob Armstrong
Lieutenant Colonel, Retired
United States Marine Corps

POSITIVE CONFLICT

TRANSFORM OPPOSITION INTO INNOVATION

Darby Checketts

CAREER
PRESS
The Career Press, Inc.
Franklin Lakes, NJ

Copyright©2007 by Darby Checketts

POSITIVE CONFLICT
EDITED BY KATE HENCHES
TYPESET BY MICHAEL FITZGIBBON
Cover design by The Design Works Group
Printed in the U.S.A. by Book-mart Press

To order this title, please call toll-free 1-800-CAREER-1 (NJ and Canada: 201-848-0310) to order using VISA or MasterCard, or for further information on books from Career Press.

CAREER
PRESS

The Career Press, Inc., 3 Tice Road, PO Box 687,
Franklin Lakes, NJ 07417
www.careerpress.com

Library of Congress Cataloging-in-Publication Data

Checketts, Darby.
    Positive Conflict : transform opposition into innovation / by Darby Checketts.
            p. cm.
        ISBN-13: 978-1-56414-959-6
        ISBN-10: 1-56414-959-5
            1. Leadership. I. Title.

HM1261.C45 2007
303.69--dc22

2007027222

Dedicated to
Durwood Canham
Inspirational High School Chemistry Teacher
Phoenix South Maountain High School (1963)

Acknowledgments

I wish to acknowledge the Career Press team. A book is initially an idea and a dream. It is not fully a book until someone actually publishes it. Then, others can join the idea and share the dream. There is nothing quite like the heft of a new book with its attractive jacket and its carefully printed pages to truly fulfill the author's own dream. Special thanks to Michael Pye, Kristen Parkes, Mike Fitzgibbon, Diana Ghazzawi, Kirsten Dalley, Kara Reynolds, and Laurie Kelly-Pye. It was Kate Henches who became my chief point of contact and principal editor; who pulled it all together. At various turns in the road, she made the book a better book. I am so grateful to you all.

I acknowledge the many schoolteachers who helped me discover the ideas and the energy inside me. I thank friends in 25 countries around the globe for teaching me the positive significance of diversity—the diversity of ideas, personalities, and cultures. Thanks to John Arnold for teaching me principles and methods that facilitate the coming together of ideas and personalities in the conference room or on the factory floor. And thank you, Steve Chandler, for teaching me the true meanings of *ownership* and *optimism*.

My family will always be my foundation and my greatest source of inspiration for moving on, doing better, and doing some good.

Finally, I thank the thinkers, the experimenters, the inventors, the dreamers, and all those who have dared to put their ideas out there to benefit us all—often under the ridicule of those who thought it couldn't be done or those who disagreed with the changes underway. It is amazing how often we discover that what we thought wouldn't work—because it didn't fit with our way of thinking—was something we simply did not understand. The conflict we experience is often superficial. What lies just beneath the conflict is the opportunity for a broader understanding that becomes a source of greater creativity.

Contents

Introduction   17

Chapter 1:
The Energy Inside   23

Chapter 2:
When Opposites Collide   37

Chapter 3:
It's Not About Taking Advantage   49

Chapter 4:
A Respect for the Origin of Ideas   57

Chapter 5:
The Huge Fallacy of Not Listening   63

Chapter 6:
The Optimist's Answer to Everything   81

Chapter 7:
Leadership: Becoming the Master of Dichotomies   101

Chapter 8:
Communication: From Conflict to Innovation   113

Chapter 9:
The Power of Personality Opposites   137

Chapter 10:
The Power of Cultural Opposites   153

Chapter 11:
The Power of Ideological Opposites   177

Chapter 12:
Getting What You Need by Helping Others Succeed   197

Conclusion:
When Sparks Fly, They Light Up the Sky   233

Recommended Reading   **239**

Index   **241**

About the Author   **245**

About *Leverage*   **249**

Introduction

Can you picture two young brothers squabbling? Their parents stand by in moderate dismay as they shake their heads and remark: "These kids are so different. They don't get along. They seldom see eye to eye. It seems as if they are constantly teasing each other." The parents may wonder if this rivalry is caused by some deep-seated jealousy or if it is just a matter of two lively boys testing their wills as young lion cubs do.

Sharon and I are the parents of four sons and three daughters. Of course, I considered all my children to be exceptional—possessing great potential. Through the years they have demonstrated that my early bias, though not totally objective, was justifiable. Six of these children fit together in pairs: oldest daughter with oldest son, then two daughters, then two sons. And, after a gap of six years, our youngest son joined the family. At a very early age, the pair of sons displayed their

17

unique dispositions toward life. One son appeared to be a "Future Engineer of America." Although he loved to romp and play, he was an especially logical problem solver and the architect of amazing wooden and cardboard creations. The other son loved mostly football and his BMX bike. These two squabbled and they teased. And yet they were a great team when it came to certain projects: The young engineer would map things out; the football player would "execute the play" and move the material. They got the job done. There was power in their "opposite" personalities—a complementary force they could unleash once they got past what often showed up as "conflict."

The Power of Opposites

These two capable boys synergistically constructed a tree house in the dry river bottom near our home. One afternoon, I happened to overhear them as they were reveling in their achievement. Then, suddenly, a loyal friend of theirs barged through our front door and exclaimed, "Come quick! Those kids who live just down the street are messing with your tree house. They are going to tear it down. Let's go. We've got to stop them!" The fledgling NFL aspirant shouted, "Yeah, let's go get'em!" The young engineer stood back and thoughtfully asked, "Just how big are they?" One had the "get up and go" to do something about it; the other had the good sense to make sure they lived to tell about it. This was the *power of opposites* in living color. Rather than for them to just "work out their differences and get over it," they had a greater opportunity to harness the energy inside their unique personalities and to create a *fusion* of ideas and talent. Today, these two brothers are great buddies and are still a creative duo with very complementary talents.

A Sign of Leadership

To recognize the potential power of opposites is a prerequisite for parental sanity and an important indication that any leader is capable of seeing beyond conflict to create that fusion of ideas and talents that is an outgrowth of human diversity. The finest of leaders become what I call "Masters of Dichotomies." The dictionary definition of a dichotomy is "a division of things into two groups that may be, or merely appear to be, mutually exclusive." **The genius of a great leader is finding the common ground that becomes the basis for a fusion of "human energy atoms" that generates previously unforeseen power.** Common ground becomes the platform for creating a common bond where the energy of once-competing ideas is combined to produce a "multiplier" effect. Here are some examples of the dichotomies leaders resolve and merge to unleash new energy....

Be firm.	Be flexible.
Be strong…and tough.	Be kind…and loving.
You must leave nothing to chance.	You must trust others and delegate.
Value self-reliance.	Value teamwork.
You must be decisive.	You must be open to the counsel of others.
Create focus and intensity to *make it happen*.	Find the balance and peace to *let it happen*.
Lead.	Follow.
Show determination.	Demonstrate patience.
Be an achiever.	Be content.
Be powerful.	Be humble.

Please study the previous table. At first, the ideas on one side of the table appear to be the opposites of the ideas on the other side. Within each corresponding pair of ideas, the idea on the left appears to compete with the idea on the right for overriding legitimacy. In fact, the real power of these ideas is in discovering the positive tension that exists between opposites. Herein lies the secret to the greater energy that can be released as these dichotomies are reconciled and fused together.

Ask an optimist, "How can you be both powerful and humble?"

The true optimist, seasoned with wisdom, will answer, "Yes."

You may respond, "What do you mean—yes?"

The answer: "I don't always know how, but I know that I must find a way, for I value both *power* and *humility* and I will not pit these virtues against each other. I will find a way to unite them. I will be *powerful* in my determination to make things happen, yet *humble* in the knowledge that I need others to help me succeed. My greatest power will come when my associates are not intimidated by me, but uplifted by my belief in them as the finest source of power to make things happen— to help unify them in the common pursuit of our goals." This is true leadership.

Positive Conflict illustrates the principles that will help you harness the *power of opposites* and turn conflict to your advantage, which is the mutual advantage that comes by working together. You will transform opposition into innovation.

Chapter 1
The Energy Inside

For the next few minutes, imagine yourself living in the late 19th century. Picture yourself boarding a train in final preparation for a long journey. After you have stowed your personal effects in the overhead bin and taken your seat, you peer out the window of your passenger car. You look toward the front of the train and notice a railway engineer as he climbs up the steel ladder on the side of the large locomotive that will pull the train to its destination. You are surprised that you do not see puffs of smoke or hear those typical hissing and grinding sounds trains make as they are readying themselves for departure.

The engineer now climbs right up on top of the huge black machine. He kneels beside a spout that protrudes from the top of the engine as he pulls a small pouch from his pocket.

You strain your eyes and focus to see what's inside the little bag. Fortunately for this occasion, your passenger car is not so far behind the locomotive that you can't see what's going on. Next, the engineer opens a small hatch on top of the spout and then, from out of the pouch, he pulls a large, bright red strawberry. You know it's a strawberry because he holds it up in the sunlight as he gazes admiringly at Mother Nature's beautiful and delicious creation. You expect him to plop the strawberry into his mouth, at which point you would wonder why he would choose to climb atop the locomotive to have his snack. To your great surprise, he drops the strawberry down the open spout and closes the hatch.

As the engineer climbs back to the ground, the train's whistle blows. In a few short minutes, the train moves slowly, steadily, and then faster. You are increasingly aware of the awesome power of the locomotive as the train surges forward. You are on your way, but you are very curious about the strawberry ritual you have just witnessed.

I remember a lecture by my high school chemistry teacher, Mr. Canham, in which he illustrated the potential power inside a mere strawberry. He told us that the atomic particles inside a strawberry (as in all things) are held together by what is called *bonding energy*. He further explained that what we know as nuclear energy generally results from splitting atoms apart. This is called *nuclear fission*. When one atom after another atom is split in rapid succession, a chain reaction occurs and enormous energy is released. He told us that if we could split apart all the atoms in a strawberry, we could theoretically power a locomotive to travel all the way to the moon. Wow! I was astonished at the thought of all that energy inside a strawberry. I wished I could simply eat a strawberry and somehow release all that energy to create a superhuman result within me.

More Powerful Than a Strawberry

I learned that even more energy can be released by fusing atoms rather than merely splitting them apart. However, this fusion process is currently limited to solar activities occurring in the universe and is so difficult to reproduce that it may never become a reality here on Earth in our time. We all know that the quest for the power of nuclear fusion is a continuous one with occasional breakthroughs that usually prove to be misleading or disappointing.

On a day to day basis, *fusion* has a simpler, less intimidating, yet powerful meaning. It is *to bring together diverse elements to form a new whole that is distinct and somehow more useful or interesting.* For example, we enjoy "fusion cuisine" in where Asian fruits and vegetables are combined with spicy Mediterranean seasonings to create a new taste sensation. We experience the fusion of music and dance styles—perhaps the patterns of classical dance set to Latin rhythms. Fusion can also mean a colorful coalition of people bringing together their creative ideas. *To fuse is to combine, to blend into a new whole, or to melt together.*

A Fusion of Ideas

This book examines *conflict* as the signal that an opportunity for fusion exists—the bringing together of people with diverse ideas, perspectives, and cultures to create a new whole, a new taste sensation, a new rhythm, an unforeseen power that is mutually beneficial.

If there is enormous potential energy inside a mere strawberry, what is the energy potential inside a person? If there is such energy inside a strawberry, what is the potential power of an idea? If we combine the force of the wind that sweeps across the Earth, all the movement of the oceans that cover the Earth, the energy of sunlight that bombards the Earth, and perhaps all the bonding power of all the atoms of everything that makes up the Earth, this immense power does not equal the power of a single passionate person with a single innovative idea that can shape the destiny of humankind. Put two or three such people together with their innovative ideas and they might rock the world—perhaps land a man on the moon, harness the power of the sun, and somehow change the course of human history in the process. These individuals may have to deal with initial conflict before the fusion of their ideas occurs. Such conflict is the sizzling manifestation of the energy inside their ideas.

The ideas of humankind make it possible for us to capture the wind, to sail with great speed upon the oceans, to plant the seeds that soak up sunlight to grow the crops that feed us all, and to harness the power of the atom. Short of witnessing some cataclysmic event, the greatest power most of us experience is the power of ideas. Inside ideas are worlds of wonder; the events that ultimately fill history books; the inventions that move mountains or pave highways through, under, and over the mountains; the technological innovations that perform trillions of calculations per second and send communication signals around the globe. The combined energy potential of the amazing system we call "Earth" is harnessed and put to work by people with the power of their ideas.

What Is the Energy Inside?

What was the energy inside Christopher Columbus's plan to sail to the edge of the Earth in search of a new land? What was the energy inside Dr. Jonas Salk's determination to eliminate the dread disease some of us remember as polio? What was the energy inside Henry Ford's vision of horseless carriages mass-produced on vast assembly lines? What was the energy inside Winston Churchill's determination to save his country from the Nazi onslaught? What was the energy inside John F. Kennedy's idea to put a man on the moon? What was the energy inside Sam Walton's goal to help ordinary folk buy the things mostly rich people could afford? What was the energy inside Martin Luther King's dream? What was the energy that flowed from Thomas Jefferson's pen to ultimately shape governments around the world? What was the energy of Susan B. Anthony's mission to increase the authenticity of the world's foremost democracy by making it more inclusive? What was the power of the ideas that built the pyramids, the Taj Mahal, the Great Wall of China, and the Hoover Dam? What was the energy that filled a billion small packages with M&Ms and tens of millions of boxes with Cheerios? What was the creative energy that composed the music of Beethoven, Mozart, Gershwin, Elvis, and the Beatles? What was the energy that made Michael Jordan jump through the air with a swoosh? What was the energy that produced *The Lord of the Rings, Little Women,* and *The Bonfire of the Vanities?* From where did the energy come that launched the *Millennium Falcon* a hundred times and the starship *Enterprise* a thousand more? From whence came the ideas to power those electromagnetic strips on plastic cards that enable the purchase of trillions of dollars worth of merchandise in every corner of the world? And what about the power to unlock the minds and release the creativity of several billion children in classrooms in every city, in every village, every single day of the week—children who grow up to be the Jonas Salks, the Susan B. Anthonys, and the Michael Jordans—children who grow up to be loving moms and dads, conscientious employees, and neighbors who help to make our communities better?

There is boundless energy inside ideas. There is boundless physical, mental, and spiritual energy inside people. Ralph Waldo Emerson once said, "Every man I meet is in some way my superior and in that I can learn of him." My own experience is that every man or woman I meet is, in some way, truly my superior. In supporting many work teams through the years,

28

I have observed that there are always, in each group, many individuals with surprising hobbies, admirable expertise, or colorful life experiences that can transfix the imagination of every other person in the group. Although I may provide some assistance to such a group, I know that if I merely change the subject and sit down, I can be helped, entertained, or uplifted every bit as much—or—more by someone else in the group who had previously been just sitting there patiently listening to me. Now it's their turn, and I am amazed by what I learn from them.

What Gets in the Way?

What gets in the way of recognizing and valuing the wonder of each person's energy and ideas? The answer is: *conflict* in its various forms. Four specific obstacles come to mind.

1. **My Idea's Better Than Yours—Maybe.** Our individual egos can lead us to one manifestation of what Stephen Covey calls the "scarcity mentality." In the world of ideas, this is the conscious or subconscious belief that there are only so many good ideas out there and Joe's or Susie's idea is not likely to be one of them. So, we judge and reject the ideas of others to make room for our own ideas, which may be superior, or maybe not. Not only does conflict arise, but there may be an underlying assumption that we need to keep looking for a better idea. The problem in waiting for the perfect idea to come along is that Joe's or Susie's

idea might have been pretty darned good and could have been put to use right away. What can be most problematic is a strange sense we sometimes have of a "mutual exclusiveness of ideas"— that it's his or her idea versus my idea, when, in fact, a wonderful collection of our ideas is available to share.

2. **Risk Aversion: Previous Experience Shows That....** Our previous experiences too often result in the "been there, done that" syndrome that presupposes that something won't work because it didn't work before. It is too easy to become nay-sayers. Conversely, our motto ought to be "Try, try again." How many experiments did it take for Edison to perfect the incandescent light bulb?

3. **Risk Aversion: Tunnel Vision.** If we don't see *big*, we won't see enough. Unfortunately, many of us had that first big idea in the third grade. Recall that picture of an earnest schoolboy or schoolgirl proclaiming some breakthrough idea as 23 other kids in the classroom laugh out loud. Many kids decide to wait 20 years before they try again. This time, they may walk into their supervisor's office with another breakthrough idea and be told, "I appreciate your suggestion, but that's really not your job." The end result is that we learn to think small to be safe. Tom Peters says, "You can't shrink your way to greatness."

4. **Comfort Zones and Priority Conflicts.** I don't know about you, but the last time I had a big idea, it required a lot of work. If the personal payoff is there or I believe I can make a difference that's worth the effort, I'll give such a new idea a try. However, a good percentage of the time, the energy potential of great ideas is not matched by the physical, mental, and spiritual energy required to make it happen. Oftentimes, we'd rather go with the flow than fly with the eagles. Our many "other priorities" represent conflicts and get in the way. We're not necessarily lazy; we're just too practical about all the other stuff we have to do.

Be a Power Unleasher

How can we excel at harnessing the power of the "human atomic energy" people represent with the power of their ideas? How can we recognize this energy, help to unleash it, and turn it to a benefit for all?

1. **See the Twinkle / Gently Fan the Sparks.** When that next suggestion is made by your 13-year-old or a work associate, simply say, "Thanks for that idea. I'd really like to think about it and then discuss it further with you."

2. **Reserve Judgment.** Most people really do not lay awake at night trying to think up stupid things

to say. Most "dumb ideas" only seem dumb at first. Once we see these ideas in a different light, we often see what we did not see before.

3. **Buy Time/Shift the Paradigm.** Thoughtfully study any new idea. Shift the paradigm from "that won't work because" to "that could work if...." This is a powerful paradigm shift that moves from *critical* thinking to *provisional* thinking. Critical thinking keeps you out of trouble. Provisional thinking opens new doors of opportunity. Combine the two modes of thinking and you're ready to take calculated risks.

4. **See BIG.** As you shift the paradigm, ask yourself, "What is theoretically possible?" Unlock and unleash. By the way, nothing is impossible, so *any*thing is. Is what? Is possible.

5. **Be BOLD.** It's the answer to everything. It's how John F. Kennedy helped put a man on the moon, how Susan B. Anthony got out the vote, how Edison shed light on the world, how your spouse saved enough money for a trip to Hawaii, and how your 13-year-old traded his old skateboard for an iPod.

6. **Share the Spoils of Victory.** Don't be afraid to admit that Joe or Susie came up with a great idea. Be their booking agent, publicist, manager, or partner. Ask them for a healthy, performance-based

fee. You'll be the key to helping their great ideas see the light of day. They'll give you something to market. You'll both make a difference and make some serious money as well.

The Energy Inside Conflict

Finally, let's fully acknowledge this composite truth: *There is great energy inside ideas and there is expanded positive energy inside conflict itself.* That which we first characterize as *conflict* is often the initial vision of an ingenious, multifaceted possibility. As people wrestle with their differences, they make new discoveries about themselves and about the ideas they so ardently champion that rarely turn out to be mutually exclusive.

Consider two teams with very different problem-solving dispositions: Team A and Team B. The members of Team A pride themselves on their level of compatibility and supportiveness. The people who comprise Team B pride themselves on their diversity and competitive spirit.

Team A holds a meeting. They list their objectives and quickly agree on a solution. They then move, in unison, from the conference room to the break room where they share pizza.

Team B holds a meeting. Before any objectives are listed, there's some kicking and screaming (figuratively speaking, of course) about the differing points of view members of the team happen to hold. Eventually, they find the common ground, some objectives emerge, and a couple of alternative solutions are proposed for final evaluation. They, too, share some pizza as a reward for "hanging in there" to get the job done.

Quite frankly, I would recommend that you bet on Team B's success in the long haul. Although I like the neatness and efficiency of Team A's approach, it can result in superficial agreement that fails to address important underlying issues. On the other hand, some intellectual wrestling usually produces a broader understanding of the issues, a wider range of possible solutions, and therefore the prospect of a more comprehensive solution with more sustainable results. In other words, when we take the time up front to wrestle through the issues and to deal with our conflicts, implementation can go more smoothly. When we gloss over our differences, we may find that the issues resurface again and again. The rehashing of old concerns and having to reinvent the wheel are both costly uses of time.

I am not recommending that your work team squabble just to broaden your perspective. What I am proposing is that we all be patient with our initial disagreements and conflicts—that we disagree in point of view and not confuse the intellectual wrestling with interpersonal rejection. In other words, we can do as the old adage says, "Fix the problem and not the blame."

Mark Twain once said, "Hold a cat by the tail and you'll learn things you can't learn any other way." Please…cat lovers, do not take offense. You would agree that it is unwise for the person and painful for the cat for one to pick up the other by the tail. However, those individuals who have done just this have quickly learned to appreciate the astonishing agility of a cat. So, Mr. Twain's point is well taken, from a philosophical point of view. By learning to deal openly and constructively with our conflicts, we come to see the potential value in opposing ideas that would have otherwise been rejected. These multiple points of view reveal multiple facets of the more comprehensive solution we can design, once we get past the squabbling and move on.

In designing our recipes for success in life, we may choose to blend diverse ingredients and tantalizing spices to create a rich stew that is far more scrumptious than plain old chicken soup.

A Chain Reaction

There's energy inside you and me. Our ideas are the proof. As we manage our conflicts and wrestle with opposing ideas, we accomplish the fusion of these. When synthesized and synchronized, our collective ideas can change the world. Together, we see the *whole* picture. All the atoms are aligned, yet reverberating, ready for a chain reaction that can rock the world. Are you ready to unleash such energy? Human creativity is the force. We will welcome it, relish it, encourage it, share it, and use it to make the world a better place. In the final analysis, one of my mentors would offer this wisdom: "Make no small goals, for these have no ability to inspire the hearts of men and women." Inspiration is *energy inside*.

It is the goal of this book that you will increase in your confidence and skill as a catalyst for unleashing the power of diverse ideas and of varying points of view to help your associates achieve the Power of Opposites. There is no greater human triumph than when a group of people cease their contentions and decide that some purpose deserves the commitment of all. Then comes the pulling together. Teamwork is strength in numbers, creativity through diversity, hard work, and some fun. Together, we will turn conflict to your mutual advantage.

Chapter 2
When Opposites Collide

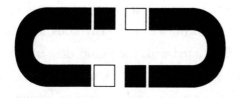

As a young man, I read and learned this verse of scripture:

For it must needs be, that there is an opposition in all things.

There is conflict built into the very design of the world and the universe of which it is a part. There are abundant contrasts. There is constant competition between opposing forces. There are countermeasures and counterbalances that humans employ. Life is very much about juggling the effects of opposites: light and darkness, health and sickness, joy and sorrow, prosperity and poverty, good and evil. With each of these opposite pairs, we seek to accentuate the one and avoid the other. Would the world and our existence in it be simpler and operate more smoothly if there were not such profound opposites? If all were darkness, sickness, sorrow, poverty, and evil, life would simply be *without any hope*. If all were light, health, joy, prosperity, and goodness, we would live in a state of idle bliss. What's wrong with that? We shall see.

Purpose

There are many philosophies about the origin and the purpose of this Earth and those who live upon it. At some point we must wrestle with possibilities. If there is no purpose, then all is temporary and of no lasting consequence that we would ever know once we go to our graves. If there is a purpose, then such a purpose is not likely to be frivolous, and there would be some goal associated with the grand design of which we are somehow a part. If that goal is to make life a meaningful experience, then the famous athlete's rationalization would most likely apply: *no pain, no gain*. Or, a more optimistic view would generally be: *You and I benefit from life in proportion to the work we put into it.*

Resistance

When I undertook body building during my high school years, I learned the basics of "resistance training." Muscles don't grow and become stronger until they meet and overcome resistance. The same principles apply in strengthening one's character. We become stronger, braver, and more capable by meeting and overcoming life's problems. Personal growth comes about as a result of the contests we encounter and the struggles we successfully endure.

The beauty of light is measured in contrast to the gloom of darkness. The blessing of health is not fully appreciated until we lose it and experience sickness. Joy is more precious as we resolve to move beyond the sorrow that is inevitable in life. Prosperity reduces the fear of poverty and may open the door to our generosity. And the reason we love Superman movies is that we love to see good triumph over evil. Superman would not be so cool if he didn't have Lex Luthor to challenge him. So, it would appear that there must be opposition in all things so that we can triumph over adversity to make life more meaningful. Otherwise, we would live without hope or we would languish in la-la land with no hurdles to overcome.

Thus we encounter conflict, day in and day out. We work with a frenzy to complete our labors while the daylight lasts and before night falls. We exercise and watch calories to avoid poor health. We learn to be brave to overcome sorrow. We attend school and work hard to avoid poverty. We aspire to leap tall buildings, fly faster than a speeding bullet, and become more powerful than a locomotive so that we can triumph over evil. Or, if our superpowers fall short, we invent the elevator and the airplane, and we build a bigger locomotive. Aren't we clever then? Look what we have overcome. Just like Superman, we have overcome the opposition of gravity, the opposition of the wind, and we can create the momentum to pull 10,000 times our own weight. We even harness the power of opposing forces. After all, it is the very same wind current that lifts an airplane into the sky that also creates the friction, which the thrust of its engines must overcome. Our success is defined by how we face conflict and overcome opposition.

Disagreements

Then there are those human-to-human conflicts we must resolve. What if everybody in the world disagreed with you and didn't want to discuss it? What if everybody agreed with you and then went their separate ways? Where would the "bond" of any relationship occur? With unending disagreement, we would all choose to become hermits. Conversely, in full and continuous agreement, we would enjoy a mere country club atmosphere that could grow tiresome.

By coming together and working to resolve our differences, we discover our individual uniqueness and talents. We ultimately discover that two heads are better than one, and then a bond grows out of our collaborative problem-solving. It's called *teamwork*. Teammates consolidate strength, cleverness, and energy to do the work of super-heroes. But, before the complementary nature of their capabilities was discovered, there was conflict. Before there was a team, there was "my way." Each member of the team had to come to grips with whether "my way is the only way" or not, and then decide to move beyond any feelings of alienation to welcome new friends, to consider their ideas, and to make of them true allies.

40

Collisions

Let's examine the collisions of life, when your ideas meet mine and there's conflict between us…or, on a global scale, when cultures clash and nations may go to war.

As an author, it is always fascinating to observe the noncoincidental nature of the inspiration that comes to help in the writing of this section or that section of a book. At this stage of writing this book, there are world conflicts of enormous proportions. There is the clash of Shiite and Sunni Muslims in Iraq. Of course, the Democrats have just taken control of Congress and presume to create a more bipartisan atmosphere in Washington. Then, the Pope announced his plans to visit Turkey with its 90 percent Muslim population. The CNN headline read: "When Faiths Collide." Finally, one news commentator said this: "Until there is conflict, there is no story." So, the question becomes: can or will these monumental conflicts be turned to a powerful advantage? Although I have no doubt that a dialogue between you (my reader) and me would help us resolve our disagreements, I am not as confident where the Democrats and Republicans are concerned, but that's not the principal focus of this book. Nevertheless, I invite you to purchase copies of this book for your representatives in Congress.

Here is the message I intend: It is not about whether the Democrats and Republicans will seize the moment to collaborate, it is about one question: Is there greater power in bringing two political perspectives together in leading our nation, or in having a single political perspective go unchallenged in determining the course we will follow? We know the answer, or at least the founders of our democratic republic did. Their intent was to broaden our perspectives and to promote a balance of power. There is a need for constructive opposition in all things to temper extremism in government. By bringing political parties together, we can incorporate that which is good in each of their platforms to achieve the greatest benefit for the citizens of the United States of America to whom the political system belongs and whose government it is. This is my message. And the same principles of collaboration and consensus-building hold true for your work team and for your circle of family and friends.

Multiple Perspectives

If we believe there is power in multiple perspectives to help bring about a morebalanced and complete view of things, we need to be less cynical about the realities of political infighting. Instead, we must continuously search for better ways to capture the positive power of such conflict in order to produce the collaborative advantage we seek! The success of conflict management begins with the will to get there and with the vision to see the improved end result that can occur after the infighting has subsided and as genuine communication takes place.

Let's examine some specific categories and examples of conflict:

o A parent and a child do not see eye to eye on the assignment of household chores.

• You and your supervisor see your work team's quarterly performance results through two different lenses. She just looks at the numbers. You understand the circumstances that contributed to those numbers, which she refuses to discuss.

o You call to see if your car has been serviced and if it is ready for you to pick up after work. The service technician says that he told you they may need the car overnight. You do not recall any such conversation.

• The sales department complains that a new product is not of sufficient quality and will result in a negative impact on customer confidence. The marketing department insists that "time to market" must override these considerations.

o You tell your teenager that a particular rock star is a disgrace to the human race, and your teenager explains that, in between concerts, this star visits youth detention centers to lecture on avoiding the hazards of drug use.

• You and your next-door neighbor argue over whether the government should be involved in legislation that enforces a particular set of family values that will strengthen society, or maintain a "hands-off" policy consistent with the idea of "separation of church and state."

43

o Your spouse claims that you never do anything together. Pointing out that you've been out to dinner twice this week makes no difference in your spouse's attitude. You go your separate ways on Friday night.

• The minister at your local church makes a controversial statement about a point of doctrine that contradicts everything your parents ever taught you. You think to yourself, "My mother would turn over in her grave, if she heard that."

o There's nearly a brawl at work as your associates debate the merits of various college basketball teams. At first it's good-natured kidding around, and then you decide some of your associates are honest-to-goodness knuckleheads.

• You attend a Department of Transportation neighborhood meeting in which representatives of the engineering department explain two alternate routes under consideration for a new freeway. Suddenly war erupts between the commuters and the nature conservationists.

o At a parent-teacher organization meeting at your local elementary school, there is intense debate about the basis for selecting library books to be purchased by funds donated by local families. The debate is about "topics of interest to children" versus "topics the local philanthropists see as important to society."

44

- You and your partner are deciding on a new floor covering for the kitchen-dining area of the older home you have just purchased. Two floor coverings have become the focus of your "friendly" discussions: wood versus cork.

o The president of your company announces a new productivity improvement program that will involve more flexible hours with shorter lunch and coffee breaks. Your coworkers see it as a ploy to squeeze more work out of the same eight-hour day, disguised by the notion of "flex time."

How many of these situations sound familiar to you? My guess is that you've participated in or witnessed each situation or one similar to it. Every one of these situations represents a "collision" of ideas where individuals and groups initially have opposing views on the issues. At first, there is discussion, and then the parties may become more polarized and defensive. Unfortunately, a combative spirit can emerge such that each opposing side perceives the need to win out over the other. Or, perhaps you are blessed to have family members, work associates, government leaders, and neighbors who are skillful in the art of negotiation.

The remainder of this book will shed light on numerous conflict situations such as those previously listed. The insight you gain will help you to fine-tune your negotiating and other communication skills to be a positive force for bringing such situations to an innovative conclusion.

Getting to Yes/Yes

A number of years ago, there was a book published with this title: *Winning Through Intimidation*. The book sold well and had a strong following. It was a "play hardball" book on how to seize the upper hand in any contest of ideas and negotiate whatever outcome you might require. Indeed, there are many situations in which strong-arm tactics win the day and shrewdness pays off handsomely.

Some folks view the world as a "dog-eat-dog" world where, if you don't seize the upper hand, you're dead meat. After all, they say, "It's a jungle out there." So, they would have us believe that it's all about dogs eating dogs, white-knuckle poker games, dead meat, and jungle warfare. These are interesting metaphors for an age when we hear much about partnerships and alliances. I do not subscribe to the *winning through intimidation* philosophy. I'm happy for the author who made millions selling the concept, but also glad the book is not currently on the *BusinessWeek* best-seller list. Conversely, I love the book *Getting to Yes*, which is a timeless classic based on more enduring principles that are consistent with what I believe it means to truly win. As we continue together in this book, you will discover that my philosophy is about "Getting to Yes/Yes." That's a double "yes" with special implications.

At the conclusion of this chapter, let me invite you to make two lists under these headings: "Conflict Situations I Encounter" and "Individuals With Whom I Have Conflict" (use their initials, if you prefer). Write these lists right here in the book or create the lists on a separate piece of paper, as you wish. Hang on to and remember these lists so you can return to reflect on each situation and individual with the expanding principles of *Positive Conflict* in mind. Recognize those "aha" insights when you will say to yourself: "Oh yeah, that happened to me. Now, I can better see what was really going on and how I can turn opposition to innovation next time."

Here is some space for those two lists....

Conflict Situations I Encounter	Individuals With Whom I Have Conflict

Chapter 3
It's Not About
Taking Advantage

As I considered possible subtitles for this book, one that gained some early traction was: "How to turn any conflict to your advantage." However, I became increasingly conscious of a particular tone coming from the word "your" that was not consistent with the intent of the book. It is too easy, in dealing with conflict, for the situation to turn into an "us versus them" or "your needs versus my needs" win-lose contest. Perhaps in certain of those "hardball" games of life, such a win-lose mindset can be rationalized. There is a simple and familiar philosophy that transcends this "winner take all" mentality, which also represents a very practical caution against gamesmanship and heavy-handedness in dealing with conflict. It is: *what goes around comes around.* To gain the upper hand is a temporary and a situational "win." One day, those who "lost to you" may become even more determined to outdo you.

Abundance Mentality

At the heart of the philosophy of *Positive Conflict* is acceptance of a principle taught eloquently by Dr. Stephen Covey. He teaches of an "abundance mentality" versus a "scarcity mentality." When you believe in the abundance of life, you believe there's enough of whatever you seek to go around. A scarcity mindset presumes that you must seize your share of limited resources and possibilities before someone else beats you to it and you find yourself empty-handed. A scarcity mentality also short-circuits the opportunity for trade-offs, compromises, and sharing the spoils of a win-win victory with others.

Undoubtedly, there are life-and-death situations in which it may be a matter of eat or be eaten, but this is rarely the case with most of the conflict situations you and I have in mind, I believe. In most of these situations, coming away with a nice piece of pie is better than losing the whole pie in some campaign to seize it all. So, trade-offs and compromises are a practical matter of survival—of getting along with other folks on the planet. Compromise does not mean you sacrifice your core values or your dignity—ever. Compromise, to put it most simply, is to remember the format of a multiple-choice exam question. There is often answer A; answer B; answer C, which may be a combination of A and B; and answer D, which may be "all of the above." You remember those exam questions. Such questions indicate that there are more possibilities than just one correct answer, or that combinations of answers may be even more complete than the one single choice you may otherwise make. Such it is in resolving most of the disagreements and conflicts of life.

Conflict…Conquest

Without an abundance mentality, it is common for *conflict* to turn into a game in which the outcome may be characterized as *conquest*. What we're really talking about here is being able to see that "big picture," which supersedes the often short-sighted need to win. When you face a conflict situation, ask yourself if there is some larger issue that transcends the immediate need to "seize the upper hand" or take advantage of the situation. It is essential to learn the difference between a true need to win *some prize* versus a "felt need" to just win at any cost. If you perceive some prize in turning *conflict* into *conquest*, ask yourself if this prize is perhaps some subordinate prize that lures you away from a grander prize that would represent a more meaningful and more powerful outcome. If there is, indeed, a grand prize worth pursuing, can that prize somehow be shared in a way that benefits all of the parties involved? Will sharing the prize expand future possibilities in some important way? On the other hand, if there is no grand prize with lasting value, the whole *conflict-to-conquest* scenario reveals itself to be simply about your ego. At this point, dealing with conflict becomes a test of wills or a contest of wits. And, now our discussion must go deeper.

If you feel you must win at all costs, you are driven by some personal need that will likely get in the way of the conflict resolution you claim to seek and even prevent the victory you think to be so important. Your "upper hand" may become self-defeating in the long run. When you encounter a conflict situation, these are important questions to ask yourself:

1. What am I trying to prove to myself and/or others? Is this the right situation in which to prove whatever it is? Might I win a single battle and lose something more important in the process?

2. Is there some underlying resentment or animosity toward those with whom I'm having the conflict? After all, the best of friends can experience disagreement and conflict and still remain friends. So this question is really about underlying negative feelings toward others that will undermine any possibility of reconciliation and compromise.

3. Has the conflict simply become a game? If so, what are the stakes in this game? What might possibly be at stake that is not immediately obvious? If you seize the upper hand now will you be forced to concede something greater in another arena at some point in the future?

If the conflict situation you're in is about your ego, about gamesmanship, or even about animosity towards others, you have a couple of choices, among others....

1. You can put this book aside temporarily and turn to other resources to help address your strong need to win and to shed some light on your competitive inclinations toward others. I invite you to visit

my Website and send me an e-mail. I will provide some initial coaching and recommend other informational resources you can use.

2. Rather than pretend that your interactions with others are solely about "the conflict" or "the issue at hand," call a timeout to put your other agenda on the table. This takes courage, but it shows that you have the presence of mind to recognize that "the issue" isn't the only issue. Here's what you say to those others: "Can we put our disagreement (our issue, our conflict) on hold for a few minutes? I want you to know that something else is going on here and I need your input."

As you are reading this, you may be saying to yourself, "Oh sure, like I'm going to say that." Well, the minute you do allow yourself to say that, you have established a new pattern of communication that demonstrates your more objective grasp of the situation. In such situations, those with whom you are communicating will prove to be mostly curious. They'll ask, "Okay, what is it?" You say, "I think our conversation could become a contest of wills and I don't want that to get in the way of what we really need to accomplish together. What do you think?" It is important that such a statement be about "your perception"—*what you think* and about "the conversation" and not about your presumption of the other person's perspective on the situation. Don't make them wrong. Don't make yourself wrong. Deal with the situation. Ask for input and then really listen. Whatever the other person says, reply with:

53

"Thank you for giving me your perspective." Now, the challenge will be to not debate or to try to immediately correct the situation. Simply ask one more question: "What do you think would help us keep our conversation focused on what is most important to each of us?"

Pre-Call

Through the years, I've learned that one of the most practical and mature communication behaviors is to talk about what you may need to talk about *before you have to talk about it.* Ideally, before conflict gets out of hand, you may say to me, "Darby, as we talk about these issues, I realize that we both have strong viewpoints and the conversation could turn into a debate. What can we do to steer our conversation in the most constructive direction? If there's anything either of us perceives might get in the way of what we're really trying to accomplish, let's address it now so that it doesn't become an obstacle later." This is to *pre-call* the situation—to recognize, in advance, what it is that might derail our conversation. This is to call the situation into *a moment of greater objectivity* than would exist if our conversation later turns into a debate with much less objectivity. This communication technique defuses much of the emotion that may be pent up and otherwise waiting to surface as disagreement and conflict later on. By this process, the likelihood is reduced that you or I will use emotion-laden beliefs and viewpoints against each other in an argumentative way.

Now, what would give you and me the presence of mind to take such a constructive and preventative tact in a potential conflict situation? The answer is: *we place more importance on getting something worthwhile done and on preserving the relationship at hand than on merely winning an argument or making a conquest.* This does take us back to square one, to where our fundamental priorities lie and to what "the big picture" is all about for each of us, individually. There may be someone reading this book who says, "But...I genuinely don't like the other person involved in this conflict and I don't care about the big picture for them. Their feelings and concerns are unimportant to me." All I can say in response is that this attitude is, indeed, a manifestation of the scarcity mentality. I invite you to consider these questions: What is it you will gain by serving yourself and not others? What is it you fear you would lose by serving them as well? In your quest to win and to succeed, is it possible that others you may serve could become your allies? Would such alliances multiply your own successes in the years to come?

Control or Influence

In conclusion, consider the powerful contrast between "having control" and "having influence." If we seek to predetermine outcomes by *controlling others*, we may, in fact, seize control, but such control is temporary. It lasts only until the conversation or negotiation is finished. Then, those with whom we have been interacting may feel undone by the situation and perhaps be resentful of our having seized the upper hand. If, instead, we engage others to "talk about what we may need to talk about" in order to set the stage for a more complete solution and a win-win outcome, we *have influence with others.* Influence generally has a more positive and lasting effect. Influence can last a lifetime. Through the genuine and skillful use of influence and persuasion, we do more than deal with issues, we build relationships that can make future problem solving easier. Former "enemies" may even become allies. In the context of this chapter, the greatest conquest may be to see the bigger picture and to conquer our own short-sightedness. The greatest success would be to achieve our goals while creating all around us a circle of influence that makes it possible to accomplish even more.

Chapter 4
A Respect for the Origin of Ideas

Ever since I was a boy, I've known the adage, "There's nothing new under the sun." I interpreted this to mean that, wherever the sun shines, there are no truly original ideas—not lately anyway. The puzzlement is that, if there are no truly new ideas, then what is innovation all about? Didn't Jonas Salk invent a totally new vaccine that eliminated a dreaded disease from the Earth? You may ask, "Isn't the iPod a brand new idea that has revolutionized personal portable entertainment and made Apple, Inc. even more powerful?"

Universal Principles

I have come to my own reconciliation of the "nothing's new" adage. It is this: There are eternal laws in motion that govern the universe. The things we call inventions and innovations are our human discoveries of those principles that

57

already operate around us, that we learn how to harness or manipulate to some greater human advantage. And how often is it true that one person's invention really builds on a thousand other "inventions" that preceded it? The iPod would not be possible without a myriad of inventions that went before it, and unless certain principles of chemistry and physics were forever there to allow such a device to exist and to function as it does. It is an appropriately humbling thought that our expressions of genius are merely reinterpretations of ageless principles and the foundational work of geniuses who came before us. So, can Apple, Inc. claim that they invented something brand new? No. There is nothing new under the sun. Apple has created a new package to convey timeless principles of chemistry and physics to us in a way that lets us capture and replay the music we enjoy. And what about the musicians who produced the music that we want to hear? Where would Apple be with an iPod and no tunes?

Whose Idea Is It?

The message here is "whose idea is it anyway?" I would propose that it is somewhat arrogant to presume that I've got an idea that is so good that it trumps your idea. My idea may not be my idea at all. Perhaps I should preface my claim to a "great idea" with this statement: "I'd like to share an idea that has occurred to me based on all the wisdom that has been shared with me through my lifetime by my mentors, by the authors whose books I've read, by inspiration that has come from many sources, by friends and work associates who have helped me learn from them, and so on."

Once we arrive at this fundamental appreciation for the shared wisdom that benefits us all from many sources through time, we are less prone to be so protective of our ideas or so quick to argue the merits of "my ideas" versus "your ideas." The greatest ideas become our "shared ideas." And what does this mind-set say about conflict? It says, "Get past it." Be grateful. Listen to the ideas of others. Soak up the wisdom. Don't discount seemingly strange new ideas until you really understand their true origin and intended purpose.

So where did the great ideas come from? If I were Steve Jobs and receiving an award for the most innovative consumer electronic device of the first decade of the new millennium, I would begin my acceptance speech with a slide listing several thousand great theorists, physicists, chemists, musicians, manufacturing engineers, electronics engineers, market researchers, the makers of competitive products (including Sony's Walkman), and more of those whose ideas and inventions span thousands of years of thinking and experimentation to make recorded sound a viable concept. And don't forget the designer of the RCA Victor gramophone. Steve Jobs may say, "I thank all of these for creating the foundation upon which the iPod could be built."

Who Owes Whom?

One of my mentors taught me that one of the most problematic mind-sets a person could hold would be this: "The world owes me...my company owes me...my family owes me."

Such an attitude leads only to arrogance and paranoia. My mentor went on to challenge me to spend time reflecting on "who I owe"—who I could probably never repay for their contributions to my success and happiness. He suggested, "Who taught you to read? What was that learning worth? If you had to write a check to your first-grade teacher for the value of her patience in helping you learn to read, what dollar amount would appear on the check?" Assuming that most of us had parents, grandparents, or guardians who nurtured us through childhood, how much do we owe them? How much do you owe that employer who hired you fresh out of school before you had other employment experience? If you have survived a life-threatening illness, how much do you owe the person whose knowledge of health and medicine helped to save your life? How much do you owe the people who plumbed the sewage system beneath the streets of the city where you live? Laugh and then don't laugh. Every time you flush the toilet, you have been rendered a great service in support of personal hygiene, convenience, and public health. You may argue that you pay your city water bill, and yet we all forget the toil of construction crews who labored in freezing weather, knee-deep in mud, probably paid a dollar an hour, some 70 or 80 years ago—those who dug the trenches where the sewer lines now lay.

Consider the knowledge and wisdom you can now claim to possess. Make a list of those who have contributed to it. Include these categories:

o Parents, grandparents, guardians, siblings.

• Spouses and life partners.

o Schoolteachers.

• Authors of books you've read.

o Creators of television programs you've watched.

• Builders of the Websites you use.

o Work supervisors.

• Training program designers and instructors.

o Coworkers.

• Neighbors who've loaned you tools and showed you how to use them.

o Religious leaders and ministers of all kinds.

• Coaches and counselors of all kinds.

o Doctors, dentists, and pharmacists.

• Community leaders with vision and a true sense of civic responsibility.

o Great philosophers and leaders whose wisdom has trickled down through the ages and found its way into the thinking of all of us.

• Spiritual sources you depend upon.

So how many ideas are truly and originally yours? You are the spokesperson for all those you have listed. Your ideas represent the wisdom they have acquired and shared with you through the years. Honor this *cascade of wisdom* that has blessed your life.

Much of success in life comes down to a matter of timeless basics that represent the collective wisdom of the ages. Always give credit where credit is due. The satisfaction you derive from acknowledging others will transcend any satisfaction that could ever come from proving "how smart you are." The bottom line is that you are at your "smartest" when you share the credit with others.

What does this respect for the origin of ideas have to do with "conflict management" and transforming opposition into innovation? It has to do with humility as we learn to acknowledge the ingenuity of those around us. When you and I have a dose of humility, we are less prone to argue the merits of ideas that, at first, seem to compete. We become more likely to see the merit that can be found in the diversity of ideas and that can be synthesized to create a more comprehensive and powerful perspective. We become the collectors and connectors of ideas.

Chapter 5
The Huge Fallacy of Not Listening

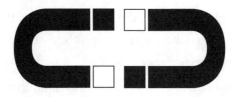

Just for fun (and for real), take a minute to list some of the dumbest things a sensible human being should really never do.

- o Drive an automobile over the edge of the Grand Canyon.
- • Eat nothing but super-sized orders of french fries, three meals a day for five years.
- o Sit on an ant hill.
- • Spit into the wind.
- o Go snorkeling at an alligator farm in the Florida Everglades.
- • _____ (add one).
- o _____ (add another).

Whatever you may have added; whatever such a list may include, there is one thing that is the dumbest of all. If you avoid doing this, you would most likely avoid the other activities on our combined list and save yourself much heartache and pain. It is this: *not listening to others.* That's a dumb thing—to not listen. We must learn to avoid "not listening." If we would listen to others, they would tell us the facts about the Grand Canyon. That famous doctor on CNN would tell us about the effects of eating excessive quantities of french fries. Those who have sat on ant hills or spat into the wind would advise us against these activities. The operator of the alligator farm would gladly explain the probability and the effects of being bitten by a 12-foot amphibian and we would avoid a painful learning experience.

It is a *huge* fallacy in life to not listen, and yet most of us encounter situations in life when we truly think we know it all. Is this ever true? Can any one of us ever know it all? I remember the comedic rationale of Steven Wright: "You can't have everything; where would you put it?" Similarly: "You can't know everything. Where would you put it...on your hard drive...in a three-ring binder...in your own private library? Even Google and Wikipedia don't know everything. There is so much to know about anything and everything that, when we proceed through life, there's always got to be an element of "winging it." Winging it means we must choose to operate on what we happen to know at the time and hope that it is sufficient. So, perhaps the question is about how much you dare to wing it. Granted, if the situation you face is whether to wash your car this afternoon or wait until tomorrow, go ahead and wing it. On the other hand, if there are lasting consequences to what you intend to do or your decision will dramatically affect others, it may be wise to seek more information. Learning from the wisdom of others and gaining their perspectives would generally appear to be a good thing.

Whose Stupid Idea Is That?

I truly do believe that people do not lay awake at night thinking up stupid things to say to each other. Even David Letterman's "stupid human tricks" are not *stupid*. They are wickedly smart because they sell tickets to his show, which lures advertisers to pay megabucks to run their commercials. Perhaps the only thing in life that is truly stupid is to decide that something is stupid before you understand what it means and why someone said it or did it. You may become convinced that the idea isn't so dumb after all, or you may initiate the dialogue that helps to improve on the idea to make it more plausible and more doable.

Imagine this: It's midnight. A woman wonders where her husband is. She gets a kerosene lantern and goes outside to the detached garage. There is her husband, Tom, holding what he calls a "carbon filament" in one hand and a glass bulb in the other. He is trying to fit the filament into the bulb without shattering it. He tells her he must seal the filament inside the bulb as he evacuates all the air from the bulb. She scratches her head and says, "Honey, it's midnight. What's with the air-tight bulb with the filament-thingee in it?" He replies, "I'm going to hook it up to this battery so the filament can glow inside the bulb without oxidizing—without catching fire. Once I get this working, you won't need that kerosene lamp anymore." She scratches her head again and says, "Tom, I love you, but that is the dumbest thing I've ever heard. Besides, you've tried something like this a dozen, maybe 100 times before, and it never works. You're supposed to be retired. If you insist on working, perhaps you should get a real job."

Another Approach

I think at some point, Mrs. Edison took a different approach. She sat down and said, "Tom, tell me more about electricity. Help me understand why this carbon filament thing glows and how it will continue to glow and glow more reliably inside that glass bulb."

Why listen?

1. To learn something.

2. To learn about others…what's important to them and how to help them.

3. It's the sincerest form of human recognition.

Whoever listened to Thomas Edison learned about electricity. They learned about the inspiration and the mission of a man who would change the world. And, they encouraged him to do so by acknowledging him and his thinking. If you claim to appreciate someone and do not have time for their *ideas*, you are quickly known to be less than their true friend. You are an imposter, as your failure to listen reveals you.

Listening: Do You Want To?

Some have said that listening is not so much a skill as it is a question of whether *you really want to* listen. If something or someone is important enough, you will listen. What if you told me you were not a good listener? I would invite you to do this experiment. Please stand over there, 20 feet away. I am now going to whisper to you three steps you can take on this coming Saturday morning that will earn you $50,000. I am only going to mention these three steps once and I will whisper as I do it. Are you ready? My guess is that you would not need to attend a seminar on listening skills. You would only need to commit your attention in accordance with the importance you assigned to the information you were about to receive or the importance of the person who was about to share with you.

My wife, Sharon, is a natural listener, not because she was born with the skills or received special training, but because she so values her relationships with those who most need to have her listen to them—our children. If our children are asked to pay tribute to their parents, they'll scratch their heads and come up with some good stuff about me, I hope. However, when asked about their mom, they'll say this: "When I was a teenager, Mom was always willing to wait up for me to come home and to sit there at the kitchen table and listen nonjudgmentally to my story and to my problems and to my excitement about the seemingly little (but not so little) things that were going on in my life." What an investment Sharon made.

The Weird-Jerk Syndrome

Let's return to the subject of *conflict*. What do we do about those who are not "Thomas Edisons" or whom we don't love as much as our kids? What about the "whackos" and those who pester us with their "dumb" ideas, taking up our precious time? What about our supposed "enemies" or those people who just seem to get in the way of our progress?

Let's talk about those "whackos" first. In a subsequent chapter, we will explore in more detail what I call the "Weird-Jerk Syndrome." Some folks out there appear to hold weird ideas. It could be said that some folks simply behave as jerks. Are we supposed to listen to them? Here's the good news. Only 6.2 percent of the residents of the average American community are actually jerks. Conversely, the chances are that, even though their ideas may seem weird in some ways at certain times, 93.8 percent of the folks you encounter are not jerks. They just say stuff you and I don't yet understand, or behave in ways that are different from our ways.

There was book written several years ago entitled, *How to Work for a Jerk*. I remember teaching a seminar and having one of the participants share this story. She said, "I bought a copy of the 'work for a jerk' book to help me understand how to get along with my boss. It wasn't long after that I was in his office and there on his desk was a copy of the same book. I couldn't help but ask him why he had purchased such a book. He looked me directly in the eyes and candidly said, 'I got it so I could learn to work with you.' I suddenly realized that we could have

68

both saved some time and money if we had just sat down and had a conversation about why we each thought the other to be a jerk."

One expert on dealing with difficult people said this: "Everybody is somebody's difficult person." How can this be? What if you are a perfectly polite, low-key, and accommodating person who is nonconfrontational and soft-spoken? How could someone think you to be difficult? Here's the answer. As a "nice person," you drive them crazy because they want you to speak up, to make your own decisions, and to provide a little intellectual give and take during your conversations together. They find it difficult to know where you're coming from. They may see you as "difficult to read and to motivate."

So, where did I get the "6.2 percent are real jerks" figure? I made it up. I think that being a jerk is in the eye of the beholder. We ascribe others to be jerks and then they live up (or down) to our expectations. At the same time, there are some people who may truly be difficult to get to know or to deal with. Most likely, they have had or are having some tough times. There may be a good reason for their outward behaviors, and if we were to ever understand what had happened to them at an earlier time or behind the scenes, we would say, "Wow. No wonder they're grouchy." Athough this may not justify their grouchiness, it may make you and me less judgmental. Consider this: *when do people need the most love?* I've been told the answer is: *When they're acting the most unlovable.* And that's when they need someone to listen to them, tough as it may be to do so.

Four Magic Words

Consider four of the most powerful words in the English language: "What is your opinion?" Here's why these words are so important. Through listening, you can turn even an enemy into an ally. Let me illustrate. Suppose there is an individual where you work who is often a negativist or a devil's advocate. Suppose you are about to make a presentation in an important meeting and he is going to be there. You dread having to deal with him. Well, I have this question: Would you rather be put on the spot in public or in private? He may take aim at you in the meeting and create a confrontation. What if you were to go to his office a couple of days before the big meeting? First of all, he'd be surprised that you bothered to come to his office, as your natural tendency had generally been to avoid him. He'd be curious. Then you say something similar to this: "Fred [we'll call your supposed adversary Fred], you are aware of the big meeting this Friday and know that I'll be making a presentation on the Aardvark project. I know you have some concerns about the cost of implementing such a project. Would you take a few minutes and tell me more about those concerns?" Fred is amazed, but, with some reserve, he begins to tell you his views. You take notes. When he is finished, you pinpoint one of his major concerns and say, "Fred, I do want to have a good way to handle this concern, just in case the problem should come up during the meeting. What is your opinion about how I could best do that?" Fred will gladly advise you.

Do you realize you have just made Fred your ally and no more your enemy? Are you ready for a miracle? As you finalize your preparations for the meeting, you will have added a flavor to your presentation that takes into account Fred's big concern. This is called "preventive action." What is more amazing is this: if anyone else raises the concern and creates a difficult situation for you during the meeting, Fred will come to your rescue. Or, as a minimum, you can call on Fred to share the very advice he gave you earlier. He is now your ally. You have transformed opposition into innovation.

The Danger of Conflict Avoidance

In the previous scenario, the "worse than" extension of not listening to Fred would have been to avoid going to his office *beforehand*. By avoiding Fred and that private confrontation about the troublesome concerns he had, you would have forced a public confrontation that would have been far more painful. What did you have to lose by asking your potential opponent for his opinion? The worst case would be that he would avoid you. This is unlikely. Or, he may meet with you and emphatically restate his opposition to your ideas. You would need to be strong. The most likely case is that he would come to realize that you were aware of his opposition and he would simply give you more background on why he opposed your ideas. He would inform you and perhaps vent a little. You would listen and learn. And, most likely, the solution you would propose in the big meeting would be a better one. Do you

71

believe this? Put it to the test. I am confident you will be amazed at the power of "What is your opinion?" About 70 to 80 percent of the time, you will experience a relationship breakthrough with someone you thought to be nearly "impossible" to deal with. About 20 to 30 percent of the time, you may hit a wall, but you'll be strong, survive your encounter, and realize that the overall odds of success are pretty darned good and that this process is better than avoiding conflict altogether.

Dealing With Difficult People

Here are some guidelines for dealing with those individuals who appear to be especially difficult...

1. **Depersonalize.** At the outset of a difficult interaction, remind yourself that the other person's concern or frustration is most likely situational. It's about "something" and not necessarily about *you.*

2. **Be agreeable.** If you can't agree *in fact*, then agree *in principle* or agree provisionally. For example, imagine that you're a financial analyst and one of your colleagues says, "The numbers in this report are wrong." Before you react, take another look at the numbers. If there is an error, agree in fact by saying, "Thank you. You're right. Glad you caught that." If you are confident there are no errors, rather than argue, say this, "I agree—if you think the numbers are inaccurate, that's a problem. Can you tell me why these numbers don't

look right to you?" **Key Principle:** A person cannot sustain anger or frustration with someone who
has just agreed with them. Had you said, "No,
you're wrong, these numbers are dead on. I've
checked them many times," you would have begun an argument. *When you fight fire with fire, you get
ashes.*

3. **Be steadfast.** Do not allow another person to be
   abusive or to violate standards of ethics, decency,
   or personal safety. Calmly remove yourself from
   the situation and/or escalate such a situation to
   your boss. If you are the boss, state your willingness
   to deal with the issue when there is an atmosphere
   of mutual respect. Ask the person to reconsider
   his or her approach, at which time you will reconsider his or her concern.

4. **Deal with issues, not personalities.** Fix the
   problem, not the blame. If someone says, "Your
   accounting department got these numbers all
   wrong," don't defend the accounting department.
   Don't make the conversation about *them.* Simply
   continue the conversation in this manner: "Can
   you please tell me which numbers appear to be
   wrong?"

5. **Let the other person finish his or her story without interrupting.** Even if you disagree with what
   is said, let it be said. Let him get it off his chest. If
   you interrupt, you will become combative and the

73

situation will deteriorate. We all know this to be true, but it is so difficult to "bite our tongues," as they say. However, once someone has let the steam out, it's mostly out. He or she be easier to deal with.

6. **Deal with specifics, not generalities.** For instance, if a customer says, "This is a stupid product design," don't argue. Ask the individual, "So that we can increase your satisfaction with the product, would you please tell me what it is, in particular, that you don't like about the design?" Here's the magic. If there's nothing specific that they can point out, they'll back off. If there is something specific, you'll be glad to know and can address it. "It" is often a relatively little thing that has them "stuck." If it's fixable, why not get them and potentially others *unstuck* on whatever it is.

7. **Take a break to buy some time.** If someone is in an argumentative or combative mode, continue to listen and focus your attention on his or her concerns (versus your likely rebuttal) *by taking notes.* When he or she has finished, say this: "I've made note of your concerns. Before I give too quick a response that may not address these adequately, I need a little time to think about the situation and get back to you." About 80 percent of the time, she'll reply, "Okay, but when will you get back to

me?" Your reply depends on the magnitude of her concerns. You may only need 10 or 20 minutes, but this is sufficient time for you to really collect your thoughts, and enough time to let her cool down and, generally, she will. Your subsequent conversation will be far more constructive.

Increase Your Listening Effectiveness by 50 Percent Overnight

Most of you have participated in various professional development programs. I have also participated in such programs. The majority of these were helpful to me at the time. However, I can only recall a handful of programs that had a vivid and lasting impact for me. The earliest of these was a two-day course on "Effective Interviewing" conducted by the University of Michigan for Ford Motor Company supervisors. I remember our instructor telling us that she was about to teach us a core skill that would transform us into 50-percent better interviewers overnight. She indicated that the teaching of the technique would require just a few minutes of our time and then we would spend the remainder of the program practicing the technique, over and over again, until it became ingrained in us. And practice we did.

Our instructor began by explaining that most of us are too good with the 5 Ws: What, Where, When, Who, Why (and How). She said that the natural tendency for most interviewers is to *probe* too quickly for details, which means one of two

75

things: (a) we presume to know what we need to know, and/or (b) we already have an agenda for where the interview is supposed to go. Both of these mindsets tend to get in the way of genuine listening. After all, a good interviewer should be primarily interested in listening. And the interviewer's principal skill should be the ability to ask good questions that prompt an interviewee to say something worth hearing.

The minute I share the *Effective Interviewing* technique, you will say, "I knew that. It's about open-ended questions versus closed-ended questions." You're absolutely right. It is that simple, but we all need a semiannual review of this principle— those of us who are parents, supervisors, counselors, good friends, supportive teammates, and so on. Our University-of-Michigan instructor taught us three magic words (as she called them): *Please tell me.* She said, "If you're really interested in knowing what's on the interviewee's mind, put him or her in the driver's seat with: *please tell me.* Otherwise, the 5 Ws point too quickly to short and simplistic answers that do not reveal much about the person you are trying to understand." To illustrate her point, if you ask someone in an employment interview what is their current job, you'll get this sort of answer: "I'm a mechanic, administrative assistant, sales rep, whatever." If you say, instead, "Tell me about your current job," some will answer in this manner: "Oh, my current job is not what I really enjoy doing. I spend too much time writing reports and not enough time face-to-face with customers. I'm in sales and had no idea there was so much paperwork." Now, that's a revealing and potentially helpful answer.

Through the years, I've found that it is helpful to turn those three magic words into four magic words instead. These are: *Please tell me about....* I discovered that people innocently cheat on the 5 Ws and say, "Please tell me what...where...when...who...why." If you add the word "about," you prevent yourself from jumping to a closed-ended question. You allow the interviewee to "comment" on a topic of interest instead of giving short, often yes or no, answers. Save the 5 Ws until you're ready to become more specific and zero in on the details. Please note here that the 5 Ws are not bad or wrong, it's about timing. Start with the lens of listening opportunity wide open with simply, "Please tell me about," and then focus more specifically with the probing 5-W questions when it is appropriate.

If you're doing a customer survey on product satisfaction, you could begin by saying, "Please tell me which of our products you like." The answer you get may be simply: "The vacuum cleaner." If it is vacuum cleaners you're ready to talk about, this is fine. Next, you can even choose to ask: "What do you like about our vacuum cleaners?" On the other hand, consider the different impact of asking a more open-ended question: "Please tell me about your experience with our products." The answer may now become: "Oh your products are great and I particularly love the vacuum cleaner. However, it's the dumb instruction manuals you guys write that confuse the heck out of me. This is what makes me buy your competitor's products." Wow! You might not have thought to ask about instruction manuals. Now, you can probe to get to the bottom of this more revealing, challenging, and important customer concern.

This is the opportunity to probe for needed details, to get beyond generalities. You can say, "Please tell me what, in particular, you find to be confusing about our instruction manuals."

By the way, if you're worried that you'll grow tired of "please tell me about," substitute any open-ended phrase to prompt further discussion, such as: "Could you give me more background on your experience with that product?" or "Please share your thoughts on the helpfulness of our instruction manuals."

Implications for Conflict Management

What are the implications here for conflict management? Allow me to switch to a "home life" example. Those of you who are parents or who were once teenagers will appreciate this. Others who are not parents or who deny ever being teenagers will still see the connection here with employee-supervisor relationships, with customer problem solving, and much more.

Picture the teenager coming home at 2 a.m., which happens to be two hours later than promised. Dad is at the front door as the youngster arrives. He swings the door open and immediately probes, "Where have you been? Why didn't you call us? Who were you with? What were you doing?" These questions just open a kid right up, especially at 2 a.m. Just kidding. These questions have the opposite effect. Rather than "open things up," this line of questioning "shuts up."

I had to practice dealing with teenagers through the years. It took some time, but I began to get it right more often. I learned, to say, "Son, it's very late. We've really been worried about you. I'd like you to tell me about your evening. Do you want to do it now or in the morning?"

When the conversation ultimately happens, I'd say, "Please tell me about last night." I remember the first time I had the presence of mind to do this. My son said this: "Dad, I tried to call you and Mom about 11:45 last night. Where were you?" Aha, he's used a "W" question on me. I've got two choices: (a) "Son, that's none of your business," or (b) "Okay, let me tell you where Mom and I were at 11:45...." (You see, **we teach people how to treat us**.) He quickly interrupted and said, "That's okay, Dad. And, by the way, I was late because I was at Kevin's house watching videos, and after I couldn't reach you to ask if I could stay later, we kept watching the videos and we all went to sleep on the floor. That's all."

In the spirit of *Positive Conflict,* we need to begin by cutting people some slack, by being better interviewers. As we share a more constructive view between us (inter-view), we will be exposed to more interesting information that will make our commitment to listen even more productive. What we learn may shed new and helpful light on a situation that could otherwise have escalated to become more of a conflict than either party deserved. Whatever conflict there may have been is likely to yield to a more positive outcome.

Listening: A Very Intelligent Act

The commitment to listen is a commitment to bring the greatest degree of our intelligence to any situation. It is the intelligence that causes us to seek the truth and to be fair to others. It is the intelligence that prompts us to find solutions rather than to win arguments.

Chapter 6
The Optimist's
Answer to Everything

It has been said that when things go wrong, you or I must have "gotten up on the wrong side of the bed." First thing in the morning, most of us do face two simple alternatives: roll over and get out of bed on the left side, or roll over and get out on the right. Even if your bed happens to be placed next to the wall, let me invite you to imagine that your bed has two sides from which you can choose. Now, let's consider a simple parable about a boy who discovered that choosing which side of the bed to climb out of was analogous to choosing the world he would live in each day.

His name was Oliver. As a young boy, he hated to make decisions. As he got ready for school in the morning, his mother would try to tell him which coat to wear. He was contrary and rejected his mother's advice. He would pull two or three coats from the closet and then sit on the living room sofa for five minutes or more agonizing over which one to put on. Eventually, his mother would just wrap a coat around his shoulders and lovingly nudge him out the door.

At the end of the day, as Oliver began to head home from school, he could not choose which friend to walk with, so he'd just walk alone. Then, he faced the horrible decision as to whether to take the short and rocky path through the woods or the slightly longer and safer route through the neighborhood instead.

As the years went by, Oliver's behavior was a constant concern for his parents. His father told him he was a "wishy-washy" boy. The most troublesome aspect of the boy's inner conflict was the moodiness that resulted from it all. One day, he'd be happy, the next he'd be sad. In the springtime, when it rained, he wished that it wouldn't so he could go outside and play ball. When it didn't rain, he worried that the flowers he and his mother had planted to beautify the yard would surely die.

Oliver couldn't decide whom he liked and whom he didn't. He'd complain about this schoolmate and then another. He wished they would treat him better, but they didn't. So, he decided he just didn't care. His studies suffered. Some books bored him. Other books he enjoyed. What he disliked most of all were the books his teacher told him to read. He rebelled at the thought that he "had to."

His father finally counseled him quite firmly, "Son, it appears that your life is stuck between a rock and a hard place. You seem to think you are darned if you do and you're darned if you don't. You should try not to be so fickle."

One night, Oliver lay in bed looking out the window at the stars. He had heard that a child could wish upon a star and the wish would come true. He liked the idea, though he didn't believe it, but he decided to try just the same. So, he wrinkled his face and shrugged his shoulders as he blurted out his wish: "Oh magic star, make it easy for me to decide so I'll never be fickle again." Oliver sighed with some sense of relief and he soon went to sleep.

In the middle of the night, a butterfly came in through the window. It flew slowly across the room and then hovered over the sleeping boy's bed. Oliver instinctively knew something was there. He opened his eyes slowly to see what it was. He was surprised, but not startled. Something about the soft glow of the butterfly was comforting to him. He blinked and the butterfly spoke softly, "Oliver, I have come to grant you your wish." Oliver sat up and rubbed the sleepy dust from his eyes. He wanted to be sure he understood what the butterfly had said. Then, the butterfly moved to the side of the room and suddenly transformed into a beautiful fairy. She introduced herself. "Hello, Oliver, my name is Merry—that's spelled with an 'e.'"

Oliver was delighted. He asked Merry to please repeat what she had said just a moment ago and she did. Then, she continued, "Oliver, for the rest of your life you will never face more than one decision each day. It will simply be the decision as to which side of the bed you'll crawl out of when you awaken in the morning. You may roll to the left or roll to right. Once you do, every other decision that day will be made for you, it is just that easy."

Oliver understood what the fairy promised and was pleased at the simplicity of her solution. At the same time, he was

83

curious about how his life would turn out if he chose left or if he chose right, so he asked her. She went on to explain, "Young man, it is good you should ask for there are rules you must know, which are these....

About Life on the Left Side....	And Life on the Right Side....
o When you get ready for school on a winter's morning, you'll have one warm woolen coat and that's all. You will be concerned that it is older than the coats the other kids have.	o When you get ready for school on a winter's morning, you'll have one warm woolen coat and that's all. You will love it because it's so soft and so comfy.
• When it's time to go home, you'll go through the woods, but you'll worry about the toothy animals that lurk in the burrows you see.	• When it's time to go home, you'll go through the woods and you'll be curious about the furry little creatures that live in the burrows you see.
o On the left side, your day will sometimes be sad, but your mother will comfort you.	o On the right side, your day will often be happy and you'll cheer up your mother as well.
• It will rain in the springtime and the sky will be dreary.	• It will rain in the springtime and the air will smell fresh.
o You will know which friends you like best, but wonder if they like you.	o You will know which friends you like best and be thankful they like you, too.
• Your teacher will give you many reading assignments. It will seem there's more reading than you have time to do.	• Your teacher will give you many reading assignments. Out of curiosity, you will read long into the night, snuggling under the covers as you do.

Merry finished her instructions. Oliver was slightly baffled. He yawned and scratched his head as he pondered. "It seems like both sides are the same, but they're different. I'm trying to figure it out."

"Oliver, it's quite simple, both sides are the same; the only difference is your own point of view. You can decide each and every morning which view of the world suits you best. It's up to you." Having spoken this truth, Merry moved toward the window.

Oliver was still trying to understand. "Merry, my dad calls me 'fickle' and I don't like it. If I choose each day to roll to the left side of my bed or to roll to the right, I won't be fickle anymore; I'll have made a decision. Merry, are there words to describe people who live life on the left side and those who live on the other?"

"Yes, Oliver, those who regularly choose left are sometimes referred to as 'pessimists.' Those who usually choose right may be known as 'optimists.' Here is something important to remember. While the words *pessimist* and *optimist* are very descriptive and can help you understand yourself, it is best that you do not put labels on other people; just call them by name. Most of them choose either left or right, from one day to the next, until they discover which side works best for them. That's their decision to make."

"Merry, is it the right thing to be an optimist and wrong to be a pessimist?"

"That's a very good question. This idea about right side or left side is not about right or wrong. The very best people sometimes choose the left side. They may even choose to be sad or mad. It is about which side works best for you as you go through each day. This is your decision to make. Oliver, I have one more thing to say. Once you choose to go left or go right, remember it is you who creates the world you'll experience that day. At times, you may deny it, but it's true. You can't put the blame on others for what you do. No one creates your world; only you." And, with that, Merry moved closer to the window.

Oliver had one more question: "Merry, what if I choose left in the morning and later I want to turn right? Can I change?"

Merry replied, "Yes you can. Simply blink your eyes as if you had just awoken once more. Tell yourself you choose to switch sides and you will." With that, the fairy transformed herself back into the butterfly and flew out the window, far from view. Oliver sprang from his bed to get ready for school.

Internal Conflict

Some of the conflicts we experience in life are internal ones as we each decide what we believe and then choose our outlooks on life. Have you ever been wishy-washy or fickle? I have. Has your mood ever swung from the left side to the right? Mine has. These are natural human tendencies. They are not right or wrong; good or bad. They reveal the inner struggle between our *safeguarding selves* and our *risk-taking selves*, which we will learn more about in a subsequent chapter. It's about that dynamic tension that comes as we are faced with choices to make.

We've all been exposed to that image of the fellow with a little angel sitting on one shoulder and a little devil sitting on the other. We know the words, "I could do this, but on the other hand, I could do that." We also know that as we resolve inner conflicts, we experience greater peace of mind. The less conflict there is going on inside us, the easier it will be to deal with the conflict outside. As did young Oliver, we must make decisions and choose what we believe will work best in each situation we face. So, what's the answer? Here are five steps we'll consider....

1. Recognize your inner conflicts—the dilemmas you face. Accept these as normal. Work to synthesize competing points of view, to see the positive overlap of ideas, and to gain valuable insight from all of the impressions you may have.

2. Choose which side of the bed to get out of. Study the rules Merry taught Oliver (in the previous table) to understand the subtle implications of the pessimist's point of view as contrasted with the optimist's point of view.

3. Resolve to not be indecisive. Face fear and choose to move forward. You may move cautiously at first, but move forward nevertheless.

4. Decide how to include others as needed.

5. Discover the optimist's answer to everything, which is YES, and learn how this works. (This will be explained in detail later in the chapter.) Make your plans and prepare to take action.

Dilemmas

What is meant by the phrase "stuck on the horns of a dilemma"? Picture a Texas Longhorn steer with those huge, wide-spread horns. We can imagine the discomfort of being stuck on one horn. What about being stuck on both? That would be a very difficult situation indeed. The Random House Dictionary says that a dilemma is a situation requiring a choice between equally undesirable alternatives. This concept can help shed more light on the inner conflicts we sometimes feel. However, to be fair, some dilemmas are not necessarily negative situations. The alternatives may be legitimately undesirable or they may simply appear to be undesirable because we don't like their implications. Perhaps we are intimidated by the change or the work that may be required of us as we choose one alternative or the other. So, let's agree in this chapter that a dilemma is a situation in which *the choice between alternatives is not easy.* The question is: How do we avoid becoming stuck on the horns of a dilemma and therefore unable to make a decision, take action, and move on?

We all know the popular use—and sometimes overuse—of the word "denial," and yet it's true that we are all probably guilty of some forms of denial. We may choose to deny that some initially uncomfortable point of view or alternative course of action may actually be a necessary thing, worthy of consideration, and perhaps even good for us. We would find it much easier to reject it out of hand. Instead, we need this simple reminder: **Reserve Judgment.** Too often, we feel pressured to act when we should simply stand back to study the situation and learn from what's inside it. For example, if you're frustrated at work because you've got plenty to do and your boss just dumped more work on you, *reserve judgment*. At first, there is nothing but turmoil inside you. You are conflicted about what to do. Should you shoulder the added burden as would a good soldier, or be a rebel and tell the boss you're too busy and that someone else will have to help out? This is a dilemma.

As we have acquired the wisdom of life, we have often discovered that, if we don't overreact, if we sit back and just analyze the situation, it's not as bad as it seems at first. Perhaps there's a way you can get help to do what your boss has just asked you to do. Or it may be that your work priorities honestly need to change. Perhaps if you had a further conversation with your boss about what's on your platter, he or she would agree to rearrange priorities so you could defer some tasks until later. Also, be willing to ask yourself, "Do I realize the true of importance of what my boss has asked me to do? How might doing it actually benefit me as well?"

Indecision and Fear

Usually, when there is indecision, there is fear. Fear is what stops us in our tracks. Then, we procrastinate. We hope for a way out or for a rescue of some sort. Let me propose that "hoping" is procrastination in disguise. And procrastination is a way to avoid dealing with the truth. And the truth is: what you want probably requires that you change something, take some risk, and perhaps take on some work you'd really rather not do.

A number of years ago, I came across a book with a stop-you-in-your-tracks title: *I Feel So Much Better Now That I've Given Up Hope.* Consider that, in nearly all situations, hoping does not change the reality of things. Having hope can represent some form of positive anticipation, and yet it is only *what you do* that actually changes the reality you experience. Don't let my practical proposition about "hope" make you sad. It's not about "giving up a hopeful outlook," it is giving up "hoping" so you can get on with the deciding and the doing. Yes, we all hold out hope for humankind—for world peace and goodwill. At the same time, we mustn't confuse this vision of better times with wishing that the need for decisive action would go away. Some of us wish for better circumstances while others are busy creating the circumstances that will bring the changes we need. I think of the young maiden who hoped that kissing a toad would produce a handsome prince. As she was busy kissing the toad, the prince passed nearby. He was bewildered at the sight and she missed the chance to catch his eye.

Facing fear may be the second most marvelous thing we humans do, because it then frees us to do the number-one most amazing thing humans do—*think*. When we think rather than fret, we find solutions and we come to realize that what we feared was the unknown. Once we write down what we fear, we can get some more data, we can get some advice, we can study the options, and we can make a plan. As we do, most of our fears go away. That which we had otherwise hoped for was something we had the ability to create. So, we decide to just do it.

Which Side of the Bed?

We learned from Oliver that the left side is the pessimist's side and right side belongs to the optimist. So what can we learn about each point of view to help us decide? The simplest explanation is just this: *The pessimist sees obstacles where the optimist sees possibilities.* You may ask, "Are there not obstacles, indeed?" Yes, but the problem is that the *pessimist* comes up against these as if hitting a 20-foot high cement wall, and that may be all that he sees—the wall.

On the other hand, being an optimist is not about living in a fairytale world of "la-la." That's not optimism. That's foolishness and naiveté. The true optimist realizes that there are obstacles, but she looks for the way around these. Perhaps you're asking yourself about just being a "realist" instead. Here's a simple analysis. If it's raining outside, a *realist* may decide to just stay in bed. The realist is not negative or pessimistic; the realist simply yields to the circumstances and does what seems feasible at the time. Being a realist sounds fine until you're in a meeting exploring creative ideas with your team and the realist proclaims, "Come on now, let's be *realistic.*" That word *realistic* can stop your team dead in its tracks. Being *realistic* is a subterfuge for taking no risks. If your optimism kicks in, you don't deny the reality that's there, but your creativity tells you the reality can change. The impossible becomes possible as your will and your work make it so.

And here is the wisdom of wisdom: In the clearest view of things, the optimist turns out to be the *true realist* because the reality is that there are unlimited possibilities for solving just about any problem you can imagine. Let me illustrate. I will quickly refresh your memory about an amazing historical event of the 20th century.

Do you remember the story of the temporarily ill-fated *Apollo 13* lunar mission that was heroically turned around by an optimistic leader at mission control? Do you remember the colonel who asked the young computer expert what the chances were that the three astronauts would return safely? The answer was that they had almost zero chance of surviving the ordeal. The colonel's response was something to this effect: "No astronauts are going to die on my watch. Let's get to work." He summoned his team to the conference room to examine the problems the astronauts faced. They soon learned that there was a shortage of oxygen in the "command module." The colonel asked why oxygen could not be transferred from the "lunar landing module" that was still attached. A member of the team explained that there was a clogged filter of some kind and no filter replacement. The optimistic team leader then issued an imperative something similar to this: "Figure out how to help the astronauts make such a filter. Don't ask from what they'll make it. Use whatever they've got on board their ship. **Failure is not an option.**"

If you were one of those three astronauts, who would you want to be in charge at mission control—a pessimist, a realist, or an optimist? The pessimist would have said, "This is really so sad. It was bound to happen sooner or later. This shows the great risk that we took with this Apollo program." The realist would say, "Let's make preparations for a crash landing. Perhaps someone will survive. We'll stand ready to help the astronauts' families and the American public deal with this tragedy. That's the least we can do." (True.) The optimist would say, "Let's get busy. There are a thousand things we still have time to try, so let's try them. We won't give up until those three guys are safe on the ground."

This true story illustrates the power of belief. Belief is different from hope. Hope is too often about an easy way out or a mystical cure. Belief is about surmounting obstacles and seeing what others don't see. Belief opens new windows of opportunity others may have left shut. Belief declares that it's not impossible until you try it and find out. And in the trying, new windows do pop open. You move closer to a solution that might work. When such windows open, you are called a genius.

When such windows open, some will call it a miracle. The miracle is the power of belief. Your genius was in not giving up. Obstacles did not deter you. You knew just enough to have faith, but not so much that you became afraid. The realist sometimes knows too much. He or she is busy making a list of a hundred reasons why "the thing" just won't work. The optimist will thank the realist for the list and set someone to work to prevent such potential problems from occurring, then put the rest of the team to work experimenting. Experiments require great faith. Thank God for the optimists among us. Their experiments expand our horizons.

Include Others

A major opportunity to expand our creativity and minimize conflict is to embrace the philosophy that two heads are better than one. In fact, it is by asking others to join our problem-solving discussions that we do discover those "unlimited possibilities." It has been my experience through the years that I can do this simple exercise with a very predictable result. I ask a room of people to undertake a simple problem-solving task as individuals, on their own, writing down as many solutions as they can think of in 90 seconds. The average number of solutions is about six. I then ask individuals to undertake the same problem as small groups and to collaborate for the same amount of time. When those groups are done, the average number of solutions per group is generally 15. With access to the expanded thinking of a small team, each person in the room has increased his or her awareness of possible solutions by 250 percent. It works every time. I make this promise: Name any problem over which you have been agonizing, give me a flipchart and 90 seconds with three to five people, and I'll triple the number of possible solutions available for your consideration.

The Optimist's Answer

One of the central themes of this book is "the Power of Opposites"—that when opposites collide, there's energy inside. As you will remember, this is about your becoming a "master of dichotomies" (more on this in a subsequent chapter). Here's how dichotomies work. These are not the same as dilemmas. With dichotomies, it's not about two undesirable or challenging alternatives, it is about two ideas or courses of action that, at first, appear to be mutually exclusive. For example, suppose you've just been put in charge of a project and your supervisor has instructed you to be sure to *be firm*—to stay on schedule and under budget. Then, in another breath, speaking about your customers, the project supervisor says, "By the way, don't forget to be *flexible* in dealing with our customers." You may be puzzled by these seemingly contradictory instructions. The pessimist would respond with: "How am I supposed to be firm and flexible at the same time?" The realist rationalizes, "I'll just explain the rules to our customers. If I have to make an exception with the scheduling or budget, my supervisor will probably understand. After all, it's easier to ask forgiveness than permission." The optimist will respond with: "How will I be both firm and flexible? The answer is: 'Yes, I will. I don't know exactly how, but I will.'" You see; the optimist begins to look for the reconciliation of these seemingly conflicting ideas. The optimist knows there is value in both firmness and flexibility and that these ideas need not be at odds.

So, what is the answer? You must be firm about *what* you set out to do and yet feel free to be flexible in terms of *how* you go about doing it. Although your supervisor may appear to have issued contradictory directives, she may have actually allowed some latitude for the actions you will take. She is concerned that you stay on schedule. That's an expected outcome. However, she didn't tell you *how* to do that. You have the option of making trade-offs and looking for process efficiencies that will let you do more in the time allocated.

Let's suppose one of your customers asks you to shorten their schedule. Assuming the directive to "stay on schedule" generally means, "don't miss major deadlines," you recognize that taking care of this one customer early is okay and may buy you some extra time for serving other customers, with more complex requirements, later on. Thus, you please your immediate customer and also increase the odds of meeting your boss's expectations in the long run.

So, the message here is to not overreact to dichotomies at their face value. Examine the possibilities that let you have your cake and eat it too. Let's go back to *Apollo 13* for a few minutes. The technicians told the colonel that there was no way the astronauts would be able to get back on a trajectory that would land them safely on Earth. He responded with, "No astronauts are going to die on my watch." They challenged him with, "And, sir, just how do you propose that we do that?" His answer might well have been, "Yes, we will." What does such an answer mean, once again? It means that he doesn't know exactly how, right at this moment, but his commitment is clear: to not *give up* until all creative energy has been expended. He'll be working through the night to uncover possibilities no one else had the faith to believe would be there. The answer YES would be the affirmation of his ultimate commitment.

I remember overhearing a conversation in which one powerful individual was asked this question in the face of an overwhelming challenge: "How can you be sure this approach will work?" His answer was: "I am not sure that it will work, but I am darned sure that I am not sure that it won't work." You may wish to read that statement one more time. This is a marvelous statement that says, "I am not giving up on my own creativity."

The Tyranny of the "Or"

In his landmark book, *Built to Last*, Jim Collins talks about "the tyranny of the *or*." We get caught up in the faulty logic that we can only do this *or* do that...that we must be either this *or* be that. The challenge is to discover "the genius of the *and.*" In other words, perhaps we can do this *and* that...we need to be both this *and* that. The tyranny of the "or" is that we cut off our noses to spite ourselves. By limiting ourselves to one side of the "or" equation, we instantly cut off half the potential ideas and half the possibilities for solving our problems.

As you know, I love those multiple-choice questions that say, "Choose a, b, c, or all of the above." So often in life we find ourselves in a conflict about "your idea" versus "my idea" when the answer needs to be "all of the above." There are elements of my idea that, when combined with elements of your idea, make for a more creative and a more complete solution. This is why I recommend to teams who are intensely engaged in problem-solving to avoid the language, "I disagree with you," or "That won't work because." Instead, use the language of "I hear your idea and I'd like to add another point of view, if I may." There is a difference between *critical* thinking and *provisional* thinking. Critical thinking examines the potential problems or flaws inherent in an idea. Such thinking is useful for troubleshooting situations to avoid pitfalls. Provisional thinking, on the other hand, is a far better methodology for stimulating creativity. It sounds similar to this: "That's an interesting idea. Perhaps it could work, if...." Do you see that little word "if"? Instead of "that idea won't work because," provisional thinking examines conditions under which a strange-sounding or seemingly problem-laden idea could be made to work—to not lose the possibilities inherent in it. Wow.

Conversely, how many good ideas do you think have been critiqued out of existence by realists who already had too much work to do and needed an excuse to shoot down the one more idea they didn't have time to investigate?

Next time somebody says, "How do you propose to do that, anyway?" Look them in the eye and say, "Yes, I do propose to do it and I'll need your help to figure out exactly how to make it work."

Idealistic and Naïve

There is a very important sideline current you will experience as you read this book and share its principles with others. There are folks who will say, "All this optimistic stuff is sometimes a bit naïve. After all, it's a cruel, hard world out there." Others will say, "This Checketts guy with his *Positive Conflict* book is just too idealistic. The world doesn't always work out so positively." And then, they'll ask, "Do you think these ideas can work?" Now you get to recall which side of the bed you chose to get out on. Here is one possible way you may choose to respond to these presumably pragmatic naysayers: "I'm not sure these *Positive Conflict* principles will work all the time, but they're at least worth a shot. What are the alternatives—to take a *can't-do* approach or to give up? I sure don't know that these principles won't work until I've applied them to find out."

Conclusion

Here's the bottom line on being an optimist: There are studies to prove that optimists are healthier and live longer than pessimists. Optimists stay married longer than pessimists. You don't even need a study to figure that one out; you can ask those who were once married to pessimists. Optimists represent lower employee turnover than pessimists. Ask those who stayed on the job what they like about their jobs. Then ask those who quit why they resigned.

And, what is the message about your day-to-day dealings with others? Would you rather go through life assuming that other people are generally "pains in the butt," or assume that other people are those upon whom you depend for success?

Would you rather go through life assuming there's mostly bad luck awaiting you, or assume that maybe there is something you can do to turn the tide of events in a positive direction? Would you rather go through life carrying a placard that reads "The end is near," or wearing a smile that says, "If the end comes, I'm ready for *whatever's next*"?

Chapter 7
Leadership: Becoming the Master of Dichotomies

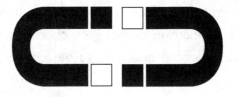

What manner of person do we envision as the ultimate leader? Who is an example you can think of as the near-perfect leader? Is he or she the person who possesses great *intelligence* and *wisdom* that comes from a wealth of experience? Is the ultimate leader also a person of great *strength* and *courage*? Together, these four qualities would represent a solid beginning to the list of virtues we might use to describe the finest of leaders. To win our full admiration, we would also expect a great leader to demonstrate both vision and compassion. Our ideal leader would have a certain charisma that would draw us to her or to him—a friendly countenance, a lively gait, and a voice that could speak with gentleness to touch us and with eloquence to inspire us. Who fits this complete description? Is it some mythological figure, some giant of history, a CEO you believe in, or a person of faith who uplifts you? Is it your father, your sister, your nephew, or your aunt who inspires you? Who is it?

Mastery

I remember the comic book characters who were the Masters of the Universe. The perfect leader would undoubtedly need some universal appeal and almost otherworldly powers to impress us and win our undying loyalty. The idea of "master" is powerful. It has biblical implications. It suggests the ultimate achievement in tennis, golf, chess, art, and music. Which violinist would not want to be schooled by a true "master"?

What have you mastered? To achieve mastery is a worthy ambition for any of us. At another level, there is the idea of self-mastery, which implies near-perfect self-control—the ability to rein in one's passions, to know when to act or hold back, to know one's strengths and weaknesses as well, to keep all things in balance. How would you rate yourself on a scale of self-mastery? I suppose we would all agree that it's a lifelong quest that may extend to eternity for all that we know. But, to master some aspect of "who we are" or some skill we possess is possible, we believe.

Most likely, you have heard a tenor or soprano sing flawlessly and leave an audience breathless. You may have witnessed a near-perfect golf game in which the player's shot seemed to ride the wind and read the movement of each blade of grass. Perhaps you have stood and looked at a painting that was sublime beyond any critique. You may have been privileged to use a product of exquisite design, unquestioned reliability, and total usefulness. You and I see signs of mastery all around us. We are both awed and intimidated at the same time. All these signs attest to the ultimate potential of humankind to learn and progress; to compete and excel. In this 21st century, we sense that we must set the mark high and reach for our best or our performance will certainly not be sufficient. Mediocrity has become even less tolerable in our technology-enhanced, fast-paced, and excellence-driven world.

Perceptiveness

My purpose in this examination of leadership is to intrigue and inspire you to do more than your best. My purpose is to lift you to see what's possible—and beyond. Of all the talents a leader may possess, perhaps the talent of the most pervasive importance would be a true *perceptiveness* about the world that surrounds us. Perceptiveness is the ability to see clearly, to see through, to see more, to see beyond what others see, and to see the truth. We have all had the experience of listening to a leader whom we admire speak words that demonstrate uncanny insight that opens our eyes as we, too, *see more* as a result. What a gift. We observe, "That's amazing. How did she figure that out? This vision she has shared changes everything. How perceptive she is."

Where the idea of conflict is concerned, many of the problems are that people do not see "more," they see less. They see no more than they want to see. They are easily blinded by prejudice. They are stopped short by laziness. Their arrogance causes them to overlook the useful ideas others possess. They see walls and not windows because of fear—fear of the unknown, fear of competition, fear of failure, fear of success, and fear that more will be expected of them than they are ready to give. It takes great courage to take off the blinders and to see all the possibilities there are. So, we sometimes retreat to what's comfortable instead and bury our heads.

As we bury our heads, we invite conflict. We become those who won't listen and prefer to argue instead. Out of such behaviors, wars are born and families are split. Our stubbornness invites conflict with those who are ready to move forward and who see our reluctance as a barrier to progress. To them, we represent a resistance they perceive must somehow be overcome. Great debates ensue. There are stalemates. No legislation gets passed. As the clock continues to tick, we lose those precious opportunities to "seize the day."

Master of Dichotomies

To perceive the energy inside conflict and the opportunity inside opposition is a rare talent, it would seem. Nevertheless, it is this talent that can break deadlocks, open doors, and move all things forward. We pray that our leader will have such an ability *to perceive*. It is one thing to perceive the obvious. It is another talent to perceive something new. But, perhaps it is most powerful to perceive *a way through*. Where others may see

104

obstacles and opposition, prepare yourself to be a *Master of Dichotomies* who sees the opportunity for nuclear fusion—the opportunity to unleash spectacular power by bonding the atoms of human creativity together rather than letting them blow apart.

Let's consider some examples and discover those methods great leaders use to master the dichotomies of life and transform opposition into innovation. Put on your leader's hat and get ready. This is important for you and for me and for those we influence. Who knows, perhaps you or I could save a marriage, elevate company morale, or help prevent a war.

Tough Love

One of the most familiar of all dichotomies is the idea of *tough love*—to somehow be tough and loving at the same time. When reconciling such dichotomies, it always helps to be sure we understand the two concepts in question. For starters, *tough* is not *rough*. Rough is like sandpaper, but tough is like leather. Rough is harsh and abrasive. Tough is strong, pliable, resilient, and therefore unbreakable. To love is to care, to nurture. To be loving and tough is to care enough to do whatever you perceive to be best for the person you love, as simple or as difficult as it may be. Thus, tough love is about strength and caring and resilient nurturing. If someone asks how you propose to be both tough and loving, you can answer, "Yes," which means, "Yes I can and yes I will find a way to be both." We know that children need to sense that the love of their parents is strong and unbreakable, and always intended to nurture them.

105

They will benefit from both the clear direction and the loving support their parents provide to them.

Theodore Roosevelt

Most American school children remember the stories of President Teddy Roosevelt. His memorable slogan comes to mind: "Speak softly and carry a big stick." This statement reminds me of Proverbs 15:1, which says, "A soft answer turneth away wrath, but grievous words stir up anger." Proverbs may be a little at odds with Teddy Roosevelt's philosophy, but herein lies a perfect dichotomy that will yield to further understanding. The dual and dichotomous message of these two statements, put into other words, is this: We all would do well to not aggravate those with whom we have dealings, and yet it is wise to be prepared to stand up for what is right and to defend ourselves if necessary. I propose that it is a great idea to give the *softer talk* an initial opportunity to work, knowing that there is some reasonable probability that our dealings with others do not need to come to the blows that would require "the big stick" or justify grievous words.

If we choose *not* to reconcile such seeming opposites, we choose to take an *off-balance* approach, clinging to one belief system without the other. If we just talk softly but carry no stick, we may be trodden over by those who talk loudly and walk brazenly over the feelings and the rights of others. Conversely, if we put aside any softness and are quick to brandish the hard and weighty stick we carry, we will be seen as combative, prompting retaliation and perhaps starting a war where no war is needed. Thus, we see the Power of Opposites and we see opposition turned to innovation in this scenario: *If someone approaches with a big stick and we speak softly at first, we may prompt a dialogue, and a better solution might emerge to avoid the battle of sticks.* And yet, we are ready for self-defense, if necessary.

Remember, to be optimistic is not to be naïve. To be optimistic is to believe that conflict can be minimized or circumvented or turned to an advantage, but to also be prepared to deal with those who would turn conflict against us. To be prepared is prudent. *Optimism is always fortified with prudence.*

Render Unto Caesar

In ancient times, the Pharisees came to Jesus and hoped to trap him in a dichotomous situation. It is said that they thought they might "entangle him in his talk." They proposed that his teachings were politically subversive—that as he taught of service to God, he was advocating nonservice to Caesar—that no one could serve both at the same time. They hoped to trap Jesus in a dichotomy. Jesus's answer demonstrated that he was the master of many things, including dichotomies. He said, "Render therefore unto Caesar the things which are Caesar's; and unto God the things that are God's." In other words, render your taxes to Caesar; render your hearts unto God. The scripture goes on to say that the Pharisees "marveled, and left him, and went their way." Out of potential conflict, Jesus drew an analogy that was enlightening to all.

A Grand Dichotomy

Perhaps the most pervasive dichotomy I have dealt with through the years working with my clients is this: Is life all about *ambition* and *achievement,* or is it about learning to be *content* with what you have and *at peace*? Here we have a great example of the "tyranny of the *or*" that Jim Collins talks about. There are, on one hand, thousands of sublime philosophical statements about *how wise is the man or woman who finds contentment and peace*. These seem to be contradicted by the motivational speeches of those "self-deterministic," knock-your-socks-off, success consultants out there, of which I am often one. However, I don't get caught up in the argument of **achievement** versus **contentment**. I give the optimist's answer: YES! Yes, you can be both a high achiever and one who is content. You can be content in knowing that you did all you could do to achieve your goals and to make a difference. You can *achieve* that which brings contentment to yourself and to others.

Consider the super high achievers, Bill and Melinda Gates. Wow! Look what they have accomplished. Their ambition and their energy are changing the world in faraway places where mothers and fathers were once frightened that their children would die of malaria. There is a new look of contentment in the faces of these parents as this fear is erased. Parents are now free to focus on the more positive things they can do to move their children's progress forward without a preoccupation with dread disease. And, do you think Bill and Melinda sit beside their fireplace with a smile of peace and some contentment on their faces knowing they made a difference? I'm sure they do. Then, they spring out of bed the next morning to pursue their great goals once again.

Herein lies the answer: Anything taken to the extreme can become an unhelpful obsession. It is those who are obsessed with climbing the ladder of success and achieving worldly acclaim that find little peace in the process. As they scurry on their way to fame and fortune, they often forget to smell the roses. Conversely, those who are totally sanguine and content may settle for a warm blanket and a full tummy and arise in the morning to ask themselves, "And what good have I done?"

The objective is to recognize where your goals and pure energy apply and to still know when to slow the pace down, to smell the roses, and to take a tender moment to read bedtime stories to your children. As you do, you will realize that you do not need to rush around the globe with a cell phone glued to your ear to find treasure. It is right there nestled in your arms. Be at peace in the moment with the ones you love best. Your goal to conquer the world can wait until morning.

Leadership Dichotomies

So, what's the secret? Here you will see, again, the table that first appeared on page 20. I invite you to seriously ponder the contrasting meanings and interpretations of each dichotomous pair following. As you do, apply the six basic steps that follow the table.

Be firm.	Be flexible.
Be strong…and tough.	Be kind…and loving.
You must leave nothing to chance.	You must trust others and delegate.
Value self-reliance.	Value teamwork.
You must be decisive.	You must be open to the counsel of others.
Create focus and intensity to *make it happen.*	Find the balance and peace to *let it happen.*
Lead.	Follow.
Show determination.	Demonstrate patience.
Be an achiever.	Be content.
Be powerful.	Be humble.

1. Define each contrasting term or phrase in the broadest sense, as we did with the ideas of both "tough" and "love."

2. Identify the merits of each of the two alternative philosophies or approaches you see. Try to understand why someone would advocate either position.

3. Look for the overlap of ideas where you may prefer one position or the other, but you can also see that some acceptable compromise could be made, *providing that....* (Here's where you use your provisional thinking to see possibilities that are otherwise blocked.)

4. Consider those individuals you admire who demonstrate the duality of leadership traits each

dichotomous pair represents. Some exemplary leaders may stand primarily for one idea or the other. Then, you will recognize those especially skillful leaders who are, in fact, true Masters of Dichotomies—those who easily reconcile the two perspectives at hand, whatever their own views may be.

5. Envision and rehearse how you would speak to and act upon either philosophy or approach.

6. See the reconciliation of the two dichotomous pairs so that you can say yes to both and discover the *Power of Opposites* that is there.

To Conclude

Among the principles of leadership that I am privileged to teach, perhaps my favorite are these: *power* and *humility*. Power is the ability to make things happen. Humility is the wisdom to know upon whom you depend for success and for strength. The greatest of leaders help to make things happen by engaging the hearts and minds of others to inspire them to heroic deeds. When the work is begun, the leader will be as the servant of all. When the work is done and the triumph song is sung, the leader will stand arm-in-arm with the team and look to the right and look to the left to say, "Look what we've done and the difference we've made, thanks to you." The greatest of heroes sees other heroes all around. Such is the power of humility.

111

Chapter 8
Communication: From Conflict to Innovation

To a large extent, this book is all about communication. It is in the context of our human communication that most conflict occurs. It is through our communication that we trigger conflict or resolve it. Many factors influence the nature and effectiveness of our human discourse. There are particular *mindsets* and a myriad of *perspectives* that we bring to our human interactions.

A Review

You will notice that the preceding chapters challenged you to examine the various perspectives and mindsets that affect your ability to deal with conflict in a constructive, even optimistic, manner. Together we looked for the energy inside conflict and examined the *Power of Opposites*, in which the fusion of ideas can unleash creativity that is otherwise blocked by prejudice.

We acknowledged the disadvantage of "taking advantage" of others, in order to encourage a broad respect for diversity and the helpful ideas of others. In Chapter 5 we began to examine communication skills with an emphasis on *listening*. The story of young Oliver illustrated principles of *optimism* and the powerful effects of such a mindset. We took the opportunity to see conflict through the eyes of those who master the art of reconciliation. We are now ready to pinpoint specific communication methods that will help to put all this into practice on a day-to-day basis.

The Art of Life

Now, let's consider in greater depth what communication is all about, including an examination of the *conceptual tools* we can use to aid us in becoming more effective communicators. It is my firm belief that of all the skills and artistic capabilities we humans can master, communication effectiveness is *the art of life*. Althou we hold great admiration for such fine art forms as dance, music, drama, painting, sculpting, and writing, there is no art form possessing a more pervasive impact than the art of communicating well. We can only begin to appreciate the day-to-day impact of those who refine *the art of relating to others*, of genuinely empathizing, of teaching, of writing, of negotiating, of influencing, of nurturing.... These are each a matter of skill and, ultimately, a matter of artistic refinement. To affirm this, we can look around at those who have worked at perfecting their communication capabilities to the *benefit of others* and in order to *get things done*.

The eloquence of John F. Kennedy was a key factor in putting a man on the moon. It was Frank Crowe whose daily instructions guided thousands of workers to create the Hoover Dam. The written words of Shakespeare have influenced countless generations. Dr. Martin Luther King's impassioned speech was crucial as he created a *tipping point* for civil rights in America. It was Secretary of State William H. Seward who influenced the United States government to make the outlandish purchase of Alaska from the Russians for a mere $7 million. The words of Eleanor Roosevelt helped our nation overcome fear and heal the wounds of war:

> *You gain strength, courage and confidence by every experience in which you really stop to look fear in the face. You are able to say to yourself, "I lived through this horror. I can take the next thing that comes along".... You must do the thing you think you cannot do."*

In a more contemporary context, I recently heard Maya Angelou deal with the dichotomies of hip-hop culture and the need for common courtesy. Her words were straightforward, compassionate, and eloquent in a way that managed to put us all on notice about vulgarity and disrespect without polarizing the many factions affected by the issue she addressed. Consider the power of words to inspire, to instruct, to entertain, to influence, and to change the course of history.

Masters of the Art of Communication

Look around you. Who do you consider to be "Masters of the Art of Communication"? Who has changed your life with his or her ability to relate, to instruct, or to somehow inspire you? When you were a child, who sat on the sofa and read to

115

you? Who taught *you* to read? Who has listened to you in a way that elevated your sense of self-worth and the value of your ideas? Who has been a peacemaker in your life—to help create understanding out of conflict? Who has helped to open your vision of the world to discover how it works? Who influenced you to take a step somewhere into your future that you had been afraid or reluctant to take? Whose words always provide clear direction or uplift you?

What do great communicators have in common? What do they do that works? If we learn these things, we will enjoy the benefits of effective communication in our everyday lives. And (in the context of this book) we will be better able to avoid the downside of human interactions, which is unproductive and damaging conflict. We will find the energy inside conflict and turn opposition into innovation.

There are libraries full of books on various communication methods. We will spend time with a number of these methods that are predominant in their impact and particularly important in transforming "everyday conflict" into *positive conflict*. Here are seven methods and commitments that will help you recall certain basics of communication effectiveness:

1. Be a reader of people.

2. Be aware of *equal* vs. *unequal*.

3. Cross the line to create rapport.

4. Deal with interests, not positions.

5. Remember the BIG picture.

6. Track your agreements.

7. Be agreeable…tell them what you *can do.*

Be a Reader of People

I remember an occasion when my dad was congratulated on a fine speech he had just delivered. His admirer said this: "Mr. Checketts, your speech was excellent. You must be well-read." My father's response was, "Thank you. In the selling profession, it has been my privilege to read many fascinating people who have taught me much." I was intrigued by the interesting twist on being *well-read.* Through the years, I have observed that the greatest of communicators are leaders who are readers of people. They recognize and honor the distinctiveness of those across the room or the conference table or even across the border. Great diplomats do not tread heavily on the cultures of others. They are intrigued and respectful of the history and the background of those with whom they must deal effectively; for the stakes are very high. (For more on cultural differences, see Chapter 10.)

If you and I wish to be competent and helpful readers of people, what are we to read about them? There is a caution here, and it is that we are not reading things into their minds and actions that are *not* there. This is obviously not the focus we would intend. *Reading* means sensing, understanding, and acknowledging the important differences in terms of where people are coming from. Examples would be evident in these situations….

o Picture a very technical software engineer explaining a sophisticated software tool to nontechnical users. Does she talk over their heads, *or* move quickly from an overview of the tool's features and functions to a clear illustration of the tool's benefits and how simple it is to use?

• If an automobile salesperson is in love with the sleek lines and speedy performance of a new model but the customer is asking questions about the lease options, does the salesperson have enough interpersonal savvy to shift the conversation to where the customer wants it to go?

o If you are sent on a diplomatic mission to meet with your counterparts in another country, do they perceive you as there to enlighten them about the superiority of your culture, or to first understand theirs?

• If your spouse is standing with arms gently outstretched as you walk through the door at the end of the day, do you hug your partner or hand him or her your coat?

Consider these three words: Rapport...Trust...Results. When we communicate with others, we do hope to achieve certain results. Those results often depend on creating some element of trust. Such trust will not occur unless there is first rapport. Rapport is the result of one person relating to another—relating in terms of that person's circumstances, cultural beliefs, practical needs, and more. Where does such sensitivity begin? It begins with silence.

Many of us, particularly in our Western culture, are very action-oriented. We want things to happen now—instantly. We drive up to the take-out window of a nearby restaurant in our fast cars to get fast food. We like to fix things. If we're sick, we want to pop a pill that will make us better instantly. We want answers.

I have been taught that great leaders learn to deal well with ambiguity. What does this mean? It means that the answers may not come fast; it means that there must be exploration before there can be discovery; it means we must listen to the other person to figure out from where she or he is coming. To be a reader of people, one must be an observer of people, which may take some time and begins with silence. Aside from the *active* forces inside us that drive us to do things, there are *receptive* forces inside us that would invite the things going on around us *to distill upon us* for greater understanding. When teaching a negotiating seminar, one of my wise friends said this: "He or she who speaks first loses." The tone of this statement may come across as somewhat manipulative at first. We infer that it means, as if in a poker game, that you do not "tip your hand." Yes, this is a shrewd negotiating technique; however, let me put a more positive and profound twist on the statement. It can also mean that she or he who speaks first speaks without insight and understanding. As we acknowledged in Chapter 5, listening is a VERY intelligent thing to do. It is a very considerate thing to do.

Next time you are in a meeting and inclined to jump right into an argument with your rebuttal, *buy a couple of minutes* of time first. Sit back and look into the faces of those in the room. See them. Hear them. Sense their energy. Sense their concern. Ralph Waldo Emerson once said, "Every person I meet is in some way my superior." Is it possible that these people with whom you may be debating are all experts in some aspect of the subject at hand, and all need to be heard before strong words of disagreement are spoken and the battle is won but the war is lost? Perhaps you will redirect your energies to facilitate the conversation and draw others out to know where they stand and to know what's truly important to them. Your contributions to the conversation relate to what they actually need and want.

Be Aware of Equal vs. Unequal

Some years ago, a methodology called *Transactional Analysis* (TA) emerged. It became very popular and is still useful for understanding interpersonal communication and relationships. The TA concepts were based on the idea that we generally approach our communications from one of three postures: Parent, Adult, or Child. When we are in our "parent" mode, we are assertive and perhaps wanting to take charge. In the "child" mode, we are playful and vulnerable. In our "adult" mode, we are working to "solve the problem." Before I continue, study this simple illustration:

Person 1	Person 2
Parent	*Parent*
Adult	*Adult*
Child	*Child*

The greatest value of this conceptual model is to guide us in recognizing the impact of interactions that are *equal* versus those that are *unequal*. To illustrate, a parent-to-parent conversation would be "equal." Such a transaction can work and, in its most positive form, would probably be characterized as a philosophical or an intellectual debate. Such a debate could become intense if two strong wills came to be pitted against each other. A child-to-child conversation would most often be both impulsive and trusting. An adult-to-adult conversation would generally be pragmatic and results-oriented. Once the two "adults" had listened to each other and begun to understand where the "other" was coming from, they could complete a very positive transaction. All this is about *equality*.

By contrast, problems occur where there are with *unequal* relationships. A parent talking *down* to a child may be an attempt to nurture the child; however (and more often than not), such a transaction easily comes across as authoritative and potentially intimidating. A child trying to "talk up" to a parent may feel weak and be in a defensive mode, and/or could be perceived as petulant and "talking out of place" to the parent. Even the best-intended interactions between a parent and an adult can easily degenerate into a "Let me tell you what I think" or "I disagree with you" or "I told you so" conversation.

The challenge is obvious and helpful, isn't it? Part of the sensitivity we hope to demonstrate is to recognize our own tendencies to be in the "parent" mode (with a tendency to lecture and scold) or to find ourselves in our "child" mode (with a tendency to become hurt and defensive). Out of such "modes" and the tendencies toward "unequal transactions" does conflict come.

Let's revisit one of the four previous examples. Consider what occurs if the software engineer says to the software users, "For you to appreciate this sophisticated software tool, you will need to take the time to understand what went into its design. Let me give you some history of how the product came about." This may sound innocent enough, but what if "the users" are now thinking to themselves, "I can't possibly understand how they design this stuff; I just know it had better be easy to use, and I hope this meeting doesn't take forever." In baseball, this would be "two strikes." Strike one: There is no relating to the audience's needs. Strike two: there is a subtle parent-child tone to the interaction. So what could the engineer say to prevent a possible disconnect? She could say, "I know how busy you all are and my principal concern in the design of this software is that it be easy to learn and simple to use. I'm here to help you get started. If any of you would like to know more of the rationale behind its design, there is a handout on the table at the back of the room, or I would be happy to take a few minutes to answer your questions." Wow! Great communicator! This is an adult speaking to those she esteems to be adults.

Cross the Line to Create Rapport

Had the software engineer not made the second statement, she would have been standing in her engineering corner of the world while her audience stood in the opposite corner somewhat intimidated by what engineers do. Furthermore, it would be as if there was a line drawn in the sand and the engineer was saying, "Now if you folks will just come on over here to understand what we engineers do, we'll get along just fine." The software users would be thinking, "Why don't you just come on over here to discover how busy we all are and why we get paranoid every time the company introduces some new software product." Some may want to draw lines in the sand for others to cross. The diplomatic approach to minimizing conflict and bringing opposites together is to demonstrate a commitment to rapport by being the first to cross whatever lines may exist to discover what's on the other side. Once this happens, trust has a toe-hold and results will be easier to achieve. In the previous scenario, the minute the software engineer said, "I know how busy you all are," she had crossed the line. There would be a subconscious sigh of relief that "she understands our concerns and wants to help us and not just promote her elegant software product."

Let me tie together three initial concepts—*being a reader of people*, *being aware of equal vs. unequal*, and *crossing the line*—with a story of my daughter, Denise, and me. She is my second-eldest daughter. She is all grown up, a registered nurse, married to wonderful Bill, and she is the loving mother of two of our grandchildren. This story takes place when she was 15 years old. One evening, when I knew Denise needed to study for a big exam that would occur the following morning, she was downstairs in our basement family room engaged in a very lively chat with a couple of her friends. Quite frankly, I wished those other teenagers would head home. I leaned over the railing at the top of the stairs in the kitchen and spoke loudly to be heard downstairs and above the youthful conversation: "Denise, it's getting late and you've got something important you need to do. Remember your big exam tomorrow." Denise had enough gumption and, quite frankly, I'm glad she dared to speak up the stairwell in response: "Dad, I *am* doing something important. I'm with my friends."

For some reason, that night, I got it. It was as if the teenage guardian angel spoke to me and said, "Okay, who's to say what's more important—exams or friends?" Here I was the 39-year-old, 6-foot-2-inch dad talking *down* the stairs in my loud voice to my young, 5-foot-2-inch daughter, presuming to tell her what I thought was most important for her. That's three *unequal* strikes. Strike one: I'm the "big ole dad." Strike two: I was bellowing down at her from the top of the stairs (not a friendly gesture to her guests, by the way). Strike three: I was dictating *her* priorities with little regard for what she thought was important at the time. Fortunately, my sudden presence of mind revealed how my behavior needed to change. I stopped talking. I went to the cupboard, found a bag of cookies, and put a half-dozen on a plate. Then, I walked down the stairs and said this: "Denise, sorry I yelled at you. I'm glad you and your friends are having a good time. By the way, I don't believe I know you guys. I'm Denise's dad. Do you want some cookies before you head home?"

Denise's friends told me their names, grabbed the cookies, and thanked me. I turned around and walked up the stairs. As I did, Denise said, "Thanks, Dad, and we'll be done in about five minutes. I'll come right upstairs and study for the exam, I promise." With my trip downstairs and that plate of cookies, I had crossed that diagonal-downward line between parent and child. I was treating Denise as one adult would treat another.

Deal With Interests vs. Positions

Do you want to see conflict in living color? Perhaps not, but for purposes of illustration, let me have you imagine a guy who owns (and loves) a Ford pick-up truck and another fellow who drives (and loves) a Chevy pick-up truck,. Ask each of them to tell you which truck is best. Now, imagine that one of these guys is from north of the Mason-Dixon Line and the other is from south of the Mason-Dixon Line. Can you see the initial sparks, hear the emotion-laden words begin to come? Feel the tension? It's going to be a heated discussion, and perhaps the conflict cannot be avoided. What's interesting here is to note that Ford, Chevy, North, and South are all *positions*—strong positions. One man stands by his Chevy, another stands by his Ford. If you were a construction superintendent and asked these two gentlemen to form a two-person task force to go buy just *one* truck for use by the company, there would be only one hope for a safe and positive outcome: The two individuals would have to somehow move from a defense of *this truck* or *that truck* to a discussion of their underlying (and even common) *interests* in choosing to drive whatever truck they might ultimately choose to buy. Let me illustrate further.

When people hold strongly to their "positions," they end up in an argument I refer to as P&C&ALH, which stands for "Pros & Cons & Argue Like Heck." A graphic analogy is that of "tree hugging." It is said that some people are so close to the trees they

125

can't see the forest. Well, some people are so close to the trees that they actually have their arms wrapped around the trees and their teeth embedded in the bark. Their opponents are standing nearby with chain saws revved up; waiting to saw down the very same trees the minute the tree huggers release their embraces. Have you ever been to a meeting, figuratively speaking, at which trees were being hugged and chains saws were humming under the conference room table? I'll bet you have. Someone has to say, "I'll put my chain saw down, if you'll stop hugging your tree."

Now, back to the two fellows with their pick-up trucks: You can see a tree labeled Ford and another tree labeled Chevy. If they are to choose just one truck for their construction crew— and even possibly consider a Dodge, Toyota, or Nissan pick-up truck, they would first need to agree to back away from their trees and then to examine their underlying interests in choosing the overall best truck to meet their collective needs. Such interests would include: drivability, ruggedness, towing capacity, roominess, reliability, fuel economy, price, styling, and so on. There would be the potential for less conflict and a more objective decision if they could agree on the most important characteristics they were looking for in a truck, and then to prioritize these. These characteristics would become the determining factors in buying not their own personal, favorite truck, but the best truck for the particular work environment their superintendent had in mind.

In life, we all find ourselves taking hard and fast positions on issues that lead naturally to conflict with others who hold different or opposing views. The secret is to avoid this line of discussion:

"Why do you like Chevys?" or "Why do you like Fords?" Instead, ask this: "What is important to you in terms of how a truck performs in the situations we have in mind, regardless of which truck we may ultimately choose—Ford, Chevy, or otherwise?"

Here's another illustration, closer to home. Suppose your partner says, "Let's go out to dinner tonight." You just finished a long commute and don't want to go out, so you reply, "I don't want to go out to dinner. I'm tired. Besides, we just went out to dinner two nights ago." Here is a classic household debate about "going out to dinner" (one position) versus "not going out to dinner" (another position). Rather than debate the reasons for going out to dinner or not, what if you simply asked your partner, "Honey, please tell me *why* you feel so strongly about going out to dinner." Imagine that she replies, "Because I just want to get out of the house and be alone with you." Now you know her underlying interests. These have very little to do with the debate over dining out and may open up new creative possibilities for your evening. You thought the conversation was about "dinner" and it's not. You may now be in the process of transforming opposition into innovation.

Real Power: Agreement in Principle

To continue the previous illustration, let's suppose you really don't want to leave the house and you'd rather eat at home. You could make some very important breakthroughs with this extension of the conversation: "Honey, if I could come up with an idea that would let us be alone without going out, would you consider it?" (This is called getting *agreement in principle*.) The response

127

is likely to be, "Well, what did you have in mind?" You reply, "How about we send the kids over to the Baxter's house for a sleepover; we order some Thai food for delivery and just spend a quiet evening home together?" She says, "I like this plan." Now, aren't you glad you got around to her underlying interests and didn't continue the argument about your opposing positions on dining out? Seriously. You might have staked your claim and never found the treasure you were seeking.

Back to Chevys and Fords: "If I can promise you the lowest priced truck with the most towing capacity and the roomiest cab, and much more, would you be willing to at least consider a Ram or a Tundra or a Titan?" We're making progress. The lens of opportunity has opened to consider many interests rather than be locked in to just two "favorite" positions.

Do you think some politicians and everyday citizens could learn from this discussion?

Remember the Big Picture

I mentioned staking your claim and never finding the treasure. We have all heard the phrase: *you may win the battle but lose the war*. When we are caught up in interpersonal conflict, we need to ask, "Is the conflict really worth it? Is this an ego thing? Is whatever the issue happens to be one of a higher priority than your relationship with your communication partners? Oftentimes, the relationship is (or needs to be) the BIG priority. Otherwise, whatever the issue is, it will never get fixed and stay fixed. Conflict often inflicts. It inflicts wounds in relationships, and then Band-Aids are used where real understanding could have resulted in a cure.

Is winning the argument about "going out to dinner" more important than being with the one you love? Is getting my daughter to study for her exam more important than demonstrating my respect for her as a young adult? Is some political agenda more important than the unity of your team or our nation? It's about relationships. If relationships are strong, there is rapport. Where there is rapport, trust begins to build. Where there is trust, results are easy to achieve.

Track Your Agreements

When a conflict arises, rather than point fingers at each other, ask how your agreement with each other is working out. Life with prior agreements is easy. Life without prior agreements is often messy. When you have previously agreed with others and things are not working out, you can both focus on what got the agreement off track and what needs to happen to get it back on track. What if you don't have a clear agreement with the other party? Stop the immediate (and potentially incriminating) conversation. Instead, take time to consider what agreement would help you better track progress in the future.

Let me go back to my interaction with Denise about the need to study for her exam. I'm going to call this "scenario #1." If she didn't know that I knew about the exam and was surprised that I was worried about it, she could have said, "Dad, I don't know why you're worried about my exam. Don't you trust me? I always study for those exams. You know I don't flunk exams." I might have responded, "Denise, you haven't flunked any exams, that's true, but it is later than usual and your friends really need to head home. I'd like you to please come up now and study." "Dad, I will, trust me." "Denise, I'd like to trust you on this, but I know that if you don't come up right away you'll be too tired to study. Come up now." Are you getting the picture of this gentle tug-of-war between Denise and I?

Here's the alternate scenario (scenario #2). At the beginning of the semester, Denise and I sat down and went over her class schedule. We realized that she had some tough science and math classes and that there would be some difficult exams. I asked her, "Denise, when it's the night before a big exam, would it make sense to start studying early and not hang out with friends too long?" She answers in the calm of the moment, "Yes, Dad. I will tell my friends they can't stay very long when I have an exam the next morning." "Denise, that's great. This is our agreement, right?" "Okay, Dad, I agree." "Thanks, Denise." Now comes that night when it's getting late and the big exam is the next morning. I walk downstairs with the plate of cookies, greet her friends, and say, "After the cookies, Denise and I have an agreement about exam night—right Denise?" "Right, Dad, I'll come upstairs as soon as we finish our cookies."

What's even more important is how our prior agreement will help us if she forgets and doesn't come right up. In scenario #1, the conversation will go this way: "Denise, why didn't you come right up like I asked?" "Dad, those are my best friends and I haven't had them over all week. Don't you trust me?" "Of course, I do, but you need to do what I ask you to do when it's this late and you haven't studied." "Sure, Dad, whatever."

In scenario #2, the conversation will go like this, if she doesn't come right upstairs right away: "Denise, what happened to our agreement about exam night?" "Dad, I'm sorry, I sort of forgot." "I understand that happens when you're having a good time with your friends, but we need to stick to our agreement. Can we do that?" "Yes, Dad, I'll do better next time. Let me go study now. Thanks." The important thing is that our conversation is about the *agreement* and not about Denise, Dad, obeying Dad, or whether we trust each other when friends are around; the conversation is about tracking the agreement we have with each other.

One of the principles that I have found to be especially powerful in guiding teams of all kinds is this: Great teams learn to talk about what they *need to* talk about *before* they *have to* talk about it. Read that again slowly. The wisdom inside this statement will begin to emerge. And what happens when great teams talk about what they *need to* talk about *before* they *have to* talk about it? They *agree in principle* as to who they are, what's truly important to the team, and how they will handle challenging situations when these arise. Ordinary teams flounder without such an understanding. They wait until stuff happens to discuss (or argue) about "who did or didn't do what and why" as the emotions run high. Life with agreements is easy. Life without agreements is often messy.

Be Agreeable

We've talked about agreements. Let's conclude this chapter by talking about what it means to be *agreeable*. A good place

131

to start is to remember the chapter on optimism versus pessimism. An optimist sees unlimited possibilities. A pessimist sees obstacles. An agreeable person is willing to go to work on the possibilities and never uses the obstacles as an excuse. An agreeable person loves the answer yes. However, she or he will not say yes if such an answer represents over-commitment. Conversely, the agreeable person rarely answers with an outright no. A no answer often represents a lack of creativity. So what if a request is made of the agreeable person for which the yes answer is over-commitment and a no answer is unacceptable? The agreeable person ACTS!

A C T stands for...

A = **A**cknowledge needs.

C = discuss **C**ircumstances.

T = **T**ell them what you can do.

Suppose a customer comes to you and says, "I know you folks promised delivery of my products in two weeks. I need them sooner, as in a week from today." You think to yourself, "This is unreasonable. We can't cut the delivery time in half, just like that." So, what do you do? You don't say yes and you don't say no. You ACT. The answer would go this way: "I understand that getting the shipment early would be advantageous and I will consider the possibilities. At the same time, the factors affecting delivery are these: Some of what you have ordered is being built to your unique specifications and there are manufacturing and test procedures we need to follow to assure the quality you expect. What I can do is check daily on

132

the progress of your particular job to let you know what the earliest delivery date might be so that, if we can improve on the original schedule, we will certainly do that. Will that help?" You didn't say yes. You didn't say no. You *acknowledged* the customer's need, opened a discussion of the *circumstances* that affect product delivery, and told the customer what you "can do." Being agreeable, in its simplest form, is being that *can-do* person. Otherwise, you may have opened a less realistic discussion about this date or that date, hoping to find one that is plausible. Quite possibly, you may have made a commitment that would only result in an apology a few days later when you and your production team realized you couldn't keep the new and more aggressive delivery commitment.

Being agreeable also works at home. Your 10-year-old comes bounding down from his upstairs bedroom and says, "I want to make brownies." You have just cleaned up the kitchen and you hate to start another mess. You could say, "No brownies; no way." Or, you could say, "Sure, go ahead make some brownies, but please leave the kitchen clean—okay?" That's a good answer. However, if you really don't want the mess, but you'd like to be agreeable without saying yes, consider this: "Son, I take it you're in the mood for chocolate. That sounds good to me; however, I just cleaned the stove and the kitchen counters and would like to keep them that way. Would some Oreos and a glass of milk do the trick?" I'll bet 50 percent of the time, Oreos will work and the mess will be less without your having to say no. The other 50 percent of the time, your discussion of circumstances may prompt this response from your 10-year-old: "Mom, I just like to cook stuff; do you know what I mean?" Now, you see the bigger picture and you agree to be even more flexible. You say, "Sure, why not. Go ahead and make some brownies."

*Oh, blessed are the flexible for they shall not get bent out of shape...*and, what's more, those who are flexible will see unlimited possibilities for avoiding conflict in the first place when there's something bigger at stake. There is a wonderful old movie starring Jimmy Stewart called *Harvey*. The character played by Stewart is a full-fledged optimist. Someone asks him why he always takes such a positive view of things. This is his answer: "When I was young, my mother told me that, in order to succeed at life, you have to be intelligent or pleasant. For the first 40 years of my life, I tried intelligent. Then, I switched to pleasant and things seem to work even better." The truth is, being pleasant is an intelligent way to approach life if you hope to enjoy it and get more out of it. Pleasant and agreeable people are quick to see the energy inside conflict and turn opposition into innovation.

The Principle of Yes/Yes

Yes is a powerful word. It is generally a door-opening, "let's move forward" word. The authors of the classic book, *Getting to Yes*, Roger Fisher and William Ury, teach us how to get that yes answer to what we need, in the context of negotiating and influencing others. At the beginning of the book, I promised to discuss the idea of getting to yes/yes. We have touched upon many opportunities for yes, including *the optimist's answer to everything*. At the conclusion of the chapter, let me illustrate what the principle of "yes/yes" means to me. It is that I will be more inclined, both consciously and subconsciously, to say yes to what you need from me as I become aware that you regularly say yes to me. I became most keenly aware of the power of this principle as I began to raise our wonderful and sometimes challenging teenagers.

I am sure that my first batch of teenage children felt for a time that dads mostly existed to say no to their children. Examples: Can I stay out until 1 a.m. tonight? No. Can I take your car? No. Can I have $20 to go to the mall? No. Can I sleep over at Susan's tonight? No. Can we buy a dirt bike? No.

I reflected on the impact my nos were probably having on my children and decided that I needed to try harder to get what I needed from them by helping them succeed. So, I initiated an experiment. The next time my teenage son asked to take my car for the evening, I said, "Yes/yes." He was delighted and puzzled. He asked, "Dad, what do you mean by 'yes/yes'?" I explained that I would say yes, if he would say yes. "Yes to what?" he further inquired. I replied, "Let's see if you can figure it out." He thought and thought and then burst forth with this: "Yes, Dad, I will be home by 1:00 and I won't stop by Bryan's house." Voila, I had new and positive leverage with my son. I had been trying to get him home before 1:00 and it had been perceived as an arbitrary parental demand, I'm sure. Now, changing his behavior was a bargaining chip in getting something he wanted even more than just staying out late. We both had interests at stake and now we were communicating about these rather than arguing about family rules. He wanted my cool car and I wanted him to be more responsible in getting home on time, and I also hoped that he would not sneak over to his hot-rod friend's house and go for a high-speed test drive in my car.

Sharon and I began teaching our upcoming teenagers the yes/ yes principle at the early and exact age of 12.5 years. They learned that the more they said yes to what parents needed, the more we said yes to what they wanted. It has worked. Someone asked me what would happen if they responded with a no answer to a request to be home on time. I explained that we would then enter "no/no" land together. I often get asked why I don't say "Yes/ but." The reason is that "yes/but" is more about my placing parent conditions on a child's behavior. "Yes/yes" is an "adult to adult" transaction in which both parties are striving to address their common concerns and mutual interests.

Yes/yes can work anywhere. Boss says, "Can you stay late tonight"? Employee says, "Sure. What do you need me to do? If I do stay late, could I perhaps take the last half of tomorrow afternoon off for my daughter's soccer match?" The president of one nation asks, "Will you please stop fishing in our coastal waters?" The president of another nation says, "Yes. Will you please loosen your trade restrictions so that we can get a better price for the fish we catch in smaller quantities as we go farther off shore?" The principles of *Positive Conflict* are intended to help us all say no and "yes/but" less often. There is more common ground for mutually advantageous solutions than we often see at the outset of whatever conflicts we may have. It is all just a test of our creativity to find a way to more than coexist—to thrive as families, as neighbors, and as allies in the broadest sense.

Chapter 9
The Power of
Personality Opposites

We've heard of the *attraction of opposites*. You noticed the two horseshoe magnets on the cover of this book. We know that such a pair of magnets can repel or attract each other. Individuals who have "opposite" personalities or dispositions may consider themselves as incompatible and too prone to competition. On the other hand, their characteristics and capabilities can prove to be complementary. It is important to differentiate between complimentary with an "i" and complementary with an "e." To compliment is to extend an expression of praise or admiration. To complement is to complete or make perfect. This is an important difference.

Personalities: To Clash or Not to Clash

When opposite personalities come together, there is potential for the conflict we refer to as a "personality clash."

Those with differing personalities may not see eye to eye. Their opinions could be polar opposites and represent little or no common ground for understanding and collaboration. If there is so much opportunity for conflict when opposites meet, what is the *attraction of opposites* all about? It's all about "getting over it," as they say. Even though conflict may occur initially, those with opposite viewpoints can certainly become engaged in genuine communication. As they do, they often discover the complementary nature of their diverse personality dispositions and realize that their opposite natures may be the basis for a more complete perspective on the issues and opportunities at hand. The fusion of their ideas can be both powerful and productive.

Through the years, I have used a particular conceptual model for understanding our various personality dispositions. We will examine this model soon. In discussing the differences in our personality dispositions with individuals and groups, one of the most-frequently asked questions is about *couples*; specifically, which relationships work best: two people together who have similar dispositions, or two people with opposite "personalities"? My answer is this: Those with *similar* personalities often have more fun but get less done. Those with *opposite* or complementary personalities may have less fun but get more done. So, each couple has the opportunity, consciously or subconsciously, to opt for *more fun* or *getting more done*. Then, if our relationships are to succeed, we must learn to love the relationships we create by acknowledging the distinct benefits they represent.

138

To illustrate, a couple with similar personalities may have similar interests and can quickly agree on recreational activities for the coming weekend. They will have a blast. As they also recognize that their yard is unkempt and their income tax return is not yet done, they can simply shrug their shoulders, smile, and say, "Don't we have fun?"

A couple with dissimilar personalities may agonize over what to do together on the weekend, but one of them has already begun planting a springtime garden and the other has all the income tax records neatly arranged on the home office credenza. This couple can rejoice in the overall efficiency and productivity of their combined skills and also decide that pursuing their individual hobbies and interests on the weekend is okay.

If these couples happen to be neighbors, one couple could share some gardening secrets and also tell their neighbors about the speedy software they use for their income taxes. The other couple could invite their highly efficient friends for a weekend of golf or skiing. This would be a neighborly form of transforming opposites into innovation.

Beyond Personalities

It is important to put the word and the idea of "personalities" into perspective. Too often, we think of ourselves and each other as having particular "personalities" or "personality types." There are two problems with this: (1) an individual may feel stuck with his or her own personality type, and (2) we may all experience the tendency to *stereotype* others by their

"personality types." The truth is that you are not stuck with
your personality because you really don't have one "type." You
are a complex and fascinating individual with your very own
philosophy of life and a collection of behavioral preferences
that are unique. You are truly "one of a kind," as is each and
every one of us. Thus, it is completely unfair to ascribe to any
individual some sort of textbook personality profile. To do so
would box us in and not allow for change and for the reinven-
tion of what our capabilities can become as we continually
grow. So, as we use the familiar terminology of "personalities," let's be sure not to turn the insight we gain about our
behavioral preferences into labels that limit the perception of
the creativity capabilities we each possess. We will look to
understand our respective personality *dispositions* in order to
more clearly appreciate the power of bringing our diverse aptitudes and capabilities together in a complementary way.

We have each acquired our so-called personality dispositions through years of employing various behaviors that have
allowed us to navigate through life with varying degrees of
success. We come to be comfortable with certain behaviors
that seem to work best for us. Notice that I use the word
"seem." Some of these behaviors are coping behaviors and
really don't solve the problem, but they let us move on. Other
behaviors are genuinely powerful for solving problems and
making progress. Add up these learned behaviors and we each
demonstrate a pattern of behaviors that some may come to
see as "personality." Thus, we talk of extroverts as contrasted
with introverts. We talk of those who are laid-back as contrasted

with those who are so-called "Type A" personalities. Then there are those fascinating combinations of personality traits: Consider the *laid-back extrovert*. He's that pleasant and talkative fellow who slouches on the couch and watches a lot of football, who can become so animated and yet still lead a somewhat sedentary lifestyle. What about the *Type A introvert?* She's the one scurrying about with her head slightly down—not saying much to those around her—as she reviews multiple checklists to be sure everything gets done. Could these two make a pair? Would the relationship last? Would they both learn and grow once they discovered the Power of Opposites? Aren't we all fascinating creatures?

Behavioral Preferences: A Conceptual Model

Here is the conceptual model to help us. Please study it briefly, and then I will address its origins and how we can use it to unlock the power of our complementary behaviors.

	Deliberate	Spontaneous
Rational	Navigator	Visionary
Instinctive	Organizer	Facilitator

This model has evolved though a period of many years since I was first privileged to meet a marvelous gentleman, the late Ned Herrmann. Ned was known for his thoughtful and highly validated theories of brain dominance. Most of you reading this book are familiar with the idea of left-brain and right-brain. We know that the major regions of our brains have distinct and complementary functions. In addition to a left hemisphere and a right hemisphere, there is the upper, cerebral region of the brain, and another region located lower in the overall brain system, which is known specifically as the limbic system. Taken together as left, right, upper, and lower regions, we surmise that there are four quadrants of brain functionality. With this in mind, the previous table will begin to make more sense as we recognize our individual abilities and propensities for utilizing a particular region of the brain in a given situation. For many of life's more complex situations, we come to realize that we will do better when we don't take a half-brained or quarter-brained approach to life. In other words, over-reliance on one region of the brain could manifest itself as a potentially limiting behavioral stereotype. On the other hand, a "whole-brained" approach would manifest the complementary nature of the multiple regions of the human brain, all working together. And, if my brain isn't tapping the potential of all four quadrants, yours may be tuned in to those other regions of the brain that will help you to help me compensate for a less-than-complete picture of the situation at hand. It's called teamwork.

It was my privilege to spend a number of days on the shore of a pristine lake near Asheville, North Carolina, being tutored by Ned Herrmann. He helped me understand and apply what he had learned about brain functionality. He granted me permission to share what I learned. I have synthesized his teachings with my own research to expand on his model and make special adaptations of it. I encourage you to visit your neighborhood library or favorite online bookstore to investigate the books he wrote. A classic is *The Creative Brain*. Ned's work has helped many to unlock the Power of Opposites as they combine their thinking patterns and behavioral preferences with those of others to create a more complete picture of the world and the opportunities out there. Such a "whole-brained" insight is important for work teams, for families, and for entire communities. Otherwise, we get bogged down in our personality clashes, in our prejudices, in the potential for pettiness, and in the game we call politics.

Please return to the conceptual model again on page 141. Look at the dimensions of the table. To simplify much of the insight about our behavioral preferences, consider that you and I and others we know demonstrate distinct dispositions along two continua: (a) from *Deliberate* to *Spontaneous* and (b) from *Rational* to *Instinctive*. Deliberate means you take time to analyze things and carefully make your plans. Spontaneous means that you like to just jump in, get your feet wet, and get going. Rational means you trust your intellect and the processes of creative thinking. Instinctive means you rely on valued traditions and you trust your "gut" feelings. When you use the four-quadrant model, you will soon see how the combination of these four dimensions of behavioral preferences lead to four distinct roles you may play in dealing with life's challenges and opportunities: You may find yourself in the role of *Navigator, Organizer,* or *Facilitator,* or you may be the *Visionary.*

One of Ned Herrmann's most important objectives was to encourage us to value all four quadrants in dealing with the world—to value a whole-brained team approach to things in business and in life. You may ask yourself as you prepare your next business plan: which of the four roles would you be willing to overlook in formulating the best possible plan and moving forward as a team? I hope none of the roles would appear unimportant to you. Now, here's the catch: You will relate to and be comfortable fulfilling one or two of these roles more than the others. This is about *your* preferences and not the importance of the various roles. A caution is to reserve judgment about those roles you do not prefer.

The *Navigator* on your team will be sure you have a map and clear directions. The *Organizer* will be sure you have a schedule, a budget, and adequate supplies for the journey. The *Facilitator* will engage the thinking of your team to build trust and harness the power of your collective ideas. The *Visionary* will see what is possible for you to accomplish and lift your sights from the footpath to see what is on the horizon. Let's now consider some of the specific issues and opportunities you will experience as you implement the understanding you gain from this model.

Where's the Pilot?

Some will ask me this: "If there's a navigator, where's the pilot?" The *Pilot* role is that of team leader, and it may be a

144

rotational role based on the situation your team faces at any given point in time. There may be times when you elect the Navigator to pilot the team because the emphasis is on a "research and analysis" phase of your work together. If a series of problem-solving meetings are needed, perhaps the Facilitator should pilot the team during that phase of your work together. And, overall, the team leader will serve as Pilot to assure that all the diverse (four quadrants and beyond) capabilities of the team are brought together to assure the most comprehensive plan and a truly synergistic outcome.

Avoiding the Weird-Jerk Syndrome

You will recall our earlier discussion of the weird-jerk syndrome. This occurs in teams, in families, and in communities when we fail to see or to remember the value of the distinct capabilities others bring to the party—or to the problem-solving process. We become stuck in our corner (quadrant) of the world and may be unwilling to cross the line, as was discussed in a previous chapter. What causes us to become stuck is that we may become fanatical about the value of our own particular corner of the world and believe that our approach is superior, to the exclusion of the opposing and yet potentially complementary perspectives other members of the team may hold. When we are fanatical, we gain a reputation for being stuck, and it's a vicious cycle of reinforcement that ultimately results in what I have called the weird-jerk syndrome. This is also when you and I are most likely to be labeled with one personality type or another. Conversely, when we are flexible and versatile, we are seen as multifaceted individuals who are able to role shift as we recognize the value in the varying perspectives others hold.

The weird-jerk syndrome is this: one person who is stuck in his or her corner sees the person stuck in the opposite corner as *weird;* the reciprocal view is that the other person is a *jerk.* This syndrome is particularly prevalent between diagonal opposites. Please refer to the conceptual model once again to consider the diagonal pairs. The Navigator may see the Facilitator as the "sweaty-palmed worrier"—too hung up on the "people problems." The Facilitator may see the Navigator as a "fine-toothed fragmentizer" who is prone to "analysis paralysis." The Organizer may see the Visionary as a "blue-sky experimenter" or "space cadet," with too many off-the-wall fantasies. The Visionary may view the Organizer as the "sure-fired old timer" who is too hung up on procedures and past traditions.

Traditions provide an excellent opportunity to illustrate the importance of crossing the line and discovering the Power of Opposites. The truth about traditions is that individuals and teams need to both *cherish* and *challenge* their traditions at the same time. There are traditions that *anchor* a team, or a family, or a community. Other traditions may become limiting and can *blind* your team and prevent you from considering new horizons. The *visionaries* on your team will see the limiting effect of traditions. The *organizers* see the importance of traditions in helping the team to be well grounded. Only when the

organizers work together with the *visionaries* will they come up
with a balanced and complementary view of your team's traditions. Initially, there is likely to be conflict between these
two groups of individuals. As they get over it, they will discover how to transform opposition into innovation. They will
choose to build on those traditions that represent your history
and your core values and to simultaneously create new traditions that will encourage creativity and adaptability in the
"brave new world."

Similarly, the Navigator and the Facilitator need each other.
The Navigator will create an excellent roadmap for your team
to follow, and yet needs someone to help the team members
gain confidence in the roadmap and get excited about the journey ahead. The Facilitator needs a roadmap as a substantive
program to teach to others in order to win their commitment
to a specific course of action. The Navigator is the reliable
mapmaker. The Facilitator is a skilled guide. A map is merely
a piece of paper if no one chooses to follow it. And it's tough
to know where to lead others if you don't have a map. Again,
the power of opposites is very evident.

Taking It to the Next Level

Here is an expanded version of the four-quadrant conceptual model. Please study it. It will help you and your team,
family, or community take the learning and insight to the next
level of practical application.

	Values	Asks	Needs	Buys	Learns From
Navigator	Accuracy	What?	Time	Price/Value	Documentation
Organizer	Predictability	How?	Clarity	Reliability	Checklists
Facilitator	Relationships	Who?	Participation	Enjoyment	Discussion
Visionary	Freedom	Why?	Space	Performance	Experimentation

As you examine the five columns, you can see how the fundamental behavioral preferences of the Navigator, Organizer, Facilitator, and Visionary play out in a variety of situations. One of my favorite illustrations of the distinctly helpful roles people play and the Power of Personality Opposites is to consider the purchasing process. Let's specifically look at the purchase of an automobile or a motor vehicle of some kind. Imagine that the leader of your organization has challenged you to be the "Pilot" and to lead a task force comprising yourself and four of your associates who possess the distinct capabilities represented by the four quadrants we've been discussing. Your specific assignment is to visit the local auto mall to select a department "staff car" for use by the team in ferrying customers about and running errands. Ask yourself these questions:

o Where will your Navigator friend go to get the facts on each vehicle needed to assure the accuracy of the map he will create? He will go to the window sticker and begin to make comparisons. He will be particularly interested in the price of the car, in its "life cost," and in the overall economic value it represents.

148

- Where will the team Organizer go to be sure the vehicle will be of sufficient quality to hold up under the hard-driving, day-to-day use to which you will subject it? She will go to the service department to check repair records and to read the warranty. She will be concerned about reliability.

o Where will your Facilitator go? He will be talking with other customers to get their opinions. He will listen to the sales pitch and consider its credibility. Then, he will go sit in the car to get a "feel for the interior" and for its user-friendliness. He will be sure members of your department will sit comfortably and enjoy driving the car.

Where will your Visionary team member go? She will go on a test drive to discover how well the car will perform in terms of acceleration, braking, cornering, and more. The automobile had better have all the latest technology to pass this test. The car must fit with her vision of what it is intended to do for the department "down the road" and into the future.

- Will your collection of experts, with their differing perspectives, produce a better decision than any one of the individuals working alone? What would be the fallacy of one of them purchasing the car without the input from others? Will there be conflict initially as they try to reach consensus?

149

Will that conflict yield to a more complete understanding of which solution is best?

You will recall an earlier discussion of two team problem-solving scenarios. Let's review. Team A is the get-along, quick-to-reach-a-consensus team. Team B is the struggle-with-the-issues, kick-and-scream-a-little team. In facing a sticky issue, Team A may go to the conference room and decide to just pick a plan and get going. We may applaud them for their smooth process and high level of cooperation. In facing the same sticky issue, Team B goes into the conference room, we hear some loud voices, and then they emerge with sleeves rolled up and sweat on their faces. They tell us their meeting is not over. They return to the room. There's more clamoring inside. They emerge to tell us they've examined many angles, done some troubleshooting, and finally agreed to move forward. On which team would you place your money?

In the two scenarios, I believe Team A will sail off into the sunset and could hit some surprisingly turbulent seas and perhaps flounder. Team B will have talked about what they needed to talk about before they hit the rough seas and they'll know what to do. As they say, "You can pay me now or you can pay me later." Paying now may be to deal with potential conflict up front and then turn the opposition into innovation. Paying later may be to gloss over the conflict and fail to find "the energy inside" that could help you deal with the obstacles you'll undoubtedly encounter down the road.

In reexamining those contrasting optimist/pessimist views of the world, we can see that the optimist views conflict as natural and as a clue to hidden treasure, as the pessimist views it as trouble and wants to avoid it. So, next time your team "hits the wall," you will call a time-out to say, "Hey, team, guess what? We've got some conflict going here. How will we handle it? What can we do to find the energy inside it and turn any opposition into an opportunity for innovation?" It is most likely that other members of the team will say, "Good idea. Let's start by giving each other the floor so that we can listen and understand the underlying interests people have and not just the outward positions we tend to take."

Principles of Team Conduct

What can your team, your family, or your community do to help you *move through* and find the power in your opposite points of view? The answer: spend some time developing your "Principles of Team Conduct" or "Team Rules." Identify some challenging situations that you are likely to face when working together. Write these down and then brainstorm some helpful ways of dealing with these situations if and as they occur. You will now be in possession of some ground rules to help guide your collective behaviors to be sure you don't flounder. This will be part of your "team agreement"—to give yourselves a diplomatic basis for reminding each other how to get back on track when disagreements occur. From the preceding paragraph we can deduce the first of your team rules....

151

Situation	Principle of Team Conduct
Situation #1: We face conflict about the issues.	Rule #1: We look for the energy inside. We listen to underlying *interests* to not get hung up on *positions*.
Situation #2: (Keep going. Add others.)	Rule #2: (Keep going. Add others.) .

Remember: **Great teams learn to talk about what they may *need to* talk about *before* they *have to* talk about it.** There is a powerful opportunity to talk with your team and/or family about the value of "whole-brained" thinking that incorporates the varied and equally valuable perspectives each of you brings to life's great adventure. Your willingness to cross the lines represented by those four quadrants (Navigator, Organizer, Facilitator, Visionary) demonstrates the versatility that will result in world-class problem-solving. Isn't that what a successful and joyful life is all about—teaming up to solve problems and then to share in the victory?

Chapter 10
The Power of
Cultural Opposites

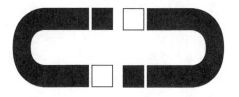

Special Note to the Reader: Much of this book contains practical methods to support your commitment to transform opposition into innovation. You will find Chapters 10 and 11 to have a slightly different tone. You might call the tone more philosophical. It is the spirit of the message that will be important in these chapters rather than the purely pragmatic elements present in other chapters. When we talk of cultural and ideological opposites, there is room for many philosophies and opinions. There are few absolute remedies. Therefore, my purpose in these chapters is to cause you to reflect on the challenges we all face in working and living together in what we have come to call our "global village." The goal is to help each of us to be constructive participants in the conversations that do influence specific outcomes, whatever these may be. In these two chapters, you will find many opportunities to refine your own approach to dealing with the fascinating cultural and ideological conflicts that are part of our everyday lives and of the world events that influence us.

As I sit here at my computer typing Chapter 10, it occurs to me that I am using a font called "Times Roman" to represent an early Anglo-Saxon language that took its written characters from the Latin alphabet. That's interesting. What's more interesting is that the numbers I'm using are "Arabic numerals." (Thank goodness we don't use Roman numerals.)

There's a little "mouse" to my right that alternates between a cursor and an arrow, similar to the arrowhead some primitive human used to kill antelope. My fingers click away on a plastic keyboard made from some byproduct of oil that was pumped from deep beneath the surface of Saudi Arabia. The whole computer thing was designed by some American scientists with software created by designers, analysts, programmers, and testers from Seattle and probably from Madras. I will soon print a copy of the virtual page on my flat-panel computer screen (made in China) onto a piece of paper invented by a Chinese fellow, named Ts'ai Lun, in about A.D. 105. He designed paper to replace bamboo, silk, and parchment, which replaced papyrus, which the Egyptians engineered.

The earliest forerunner of my printer with its "moveable type" was invented by a German fellow named Johann

Gutenberg nearly 14 centuries after Ts'ai Lun presented Emperor Ho Ti with the first samples of paper. It is interesting that my American education taught me much about Johann Gutenberg, but there was never a mention of Ts'ai Lun. Although the invention of the printing press made written materials available to the masses of humanity, which revolutionized the processes of communication and education, some historians consider the invention of paper to be more significant. Without paper as we know it, the concept of a printing press would never have occurred to its inventor. The mass production of documents would not have been feasible without a plentiful, affordable, and durable medium upon which to print.

To realize how marvelous an invention paper is, try this experiment: Go outside your house or apartment and cut a tiny branch from a tree. Peel the bark off the branch so the wood pulp is exposed. Shred some of the pulp and take it into the kitchen. Put the pulp into a blender (Ts'ai Lun didn't have one of these) with some chemicals (you figure out which ones) and blend the whole concoction together. Next, pour the whitish-yellowish goop out onto the counter. Roll the strange-smelling stuff out flat as you would a pie crust. Finally, slide the flattened goop onto a cookie sheet. Bake it in the oven at 425 degrees for 30 minutes. Remove it from the oven. When it has cooled to room temperature, go put it inside your laser printer. Hit "print" and see what happens. (Remember, you're used to printing on a perfectly uniform sheet of something with no specks or flecks that can bend and fold and survive the technological maze inside your printer....Oops.)

155

Be Thankful!

Here's some further history about the invention of paper. Its use became widespread in China during the second century. Eventually, the Chinese began exporting paper to other parts of Asia. They tried to keep the process of papermaking a secret, however, in about 751, a group of Chinese papermakers were taken captive by the Arabs. Soon paper was being manufactured in Samarkand and Baghdad. Very interesting. Then, in the 12th century, papermaking spread from the Arab world to Europe, and guess who figured out how cool paper was and decided to put it to wider use in the manufacture of books. Answer: Mr. Gutenberg, whose most ambitious project was the printing of the Bible. So, those who enjoy holding that impressive family bible in your hands as you read to your grandchildren should thank....

- ○ Johann Gutenberg for finding an affordable way to print many copies
- ● Ts'ai Lun for inventing the paper
- ○ A group of Arab merchants for capturing a group of Chinese papermakers, and who then apparently set up the first paper-manufacturing operation in Baghdad
- ● The Egyptians who gave us the idea for paper in the first place, even though their original papyrus was too expensive and perishable for everyday use.

And, don't forget to thank Mother Nature for the trees from which paper comes.

What Does It All Mean?

Here's what I conclude from this short course on the history of word processing, paper making, and printing technology: Somewhere in the Middle East, a journalist is typing a criticism of Western culture, as an American journalist writes a commentary on the cultural upheavals in Iraq. Both are using computers (word processors) invented in "the West." Both will print drafts for their editors on paper invented in "the East." The bottom line is that anyone who claims cultural superiority in this amazingly complex and interdependent world of ours is downright arrogant, I do believe. Thank goodness for the many cultures and the many inventions of the world that have come together to make this book of mine possible. Furthermore, I hope those in "the West" and those in "the East" all benefit from reading about *transforming opposition into innovation*.

I chuckle (a thoughtful chuckle) to myself when I hear those in "the East" criticize *Western culture* and those in "the West" proclaim its virtues, when the actual roots of Western civilization began in what is now the Middle East. So maybe the Middle East is supposed to be halfway between the Far East and the West. Is there an opportunity here?

Geopolitics

This is the perfect point at which to broaden the discussion of cultural opposites. As I do, I also wish to offer this important disclaimer. Most of you who are reading this book would probably agree that we are witnessing some very significant and worrisome cultural conflicts at this time in the world's history. As much as I would like to think that this book could have an impact on the myriad cross-cultural discussions and negotiations that are going on (or not going on and could be), I doubt those who are involved will get copies of the book in a timely manner. As much as you might wonder if I have a proposal for how to resolve these tragic conflicts with such far-reaching ramifications, I don't. As much of an optimist as I am, I realize that these conflicts are the result of centuries-old rivalries that have spawned much resentment and hatred, which will not easily yield to any formula found in any book. The resolution of these conflicts will require a seemingly miraculous change of heart for the millions of people who are involved on all sides of the conflict. I will continue to pray for them. My hope is that we will all encourage our leaders to be catalysts for helping others see beyond the anger and the danger of the conflict to some recognition of the underlying interests that can yet be reconciled. There are solutions that can avoid the total loss of that which is good in even the most troubled regions of the world.

Culture

Culture....What is it? What is it all about? The dictionary definition that applies here is "a particular form or stage of civilization." To broaden the definition, we think of a civilization as a collection of people with some level of philosophical, political, or technological advancement in common. As

158

civilizations advance, historians have chosen to refer to their stages as *a culture*—as an Egyptian culture or a Greek culture or an American culture. Through time, we have expanded our considerations of culture further to include the ideas of ethnic culture, religious culture, national culture, corporate culture, even community or neighborhood culture, and so on. There are implications of these cultures for purposes of transforming opposition into innovation.

Ethnic Culture

When I was a senior in high school, my dad became involved in a land development business in Hawaii. He traveled back and forth to the islands and fell in love with the beauty of the place, the clean air, and the people. I remember when he announced that we would be packing up and moving to Hilo. I was just finishing school and was heavily involved in student government and other activities. I also had a girlfriend. So, I was not a happy camper when I learned of our impending relocation. Nevertheless, I joined in to help my parents prepare to move our family of 10 from our small ranch in Phoenix, Arizona, to those faraway Pacific islands.

The home my parents had leased in Hilo would not be ready immediately, so my folks arranged for temporary housing right on the waterfront. The house was a very humble, two-bedroom, wooden-shingled structure that must have been 80 years old. It was built on short stilts to keep the seawater out. The floorboards creaked. We were very cramped for space. However, right outside the front door was the beach and the gorgeous blue ocean. The evening of our arrival, we had a dinner consisting of just fruit—more fruit than I had eaten in the previous six months. I came to discover that, in Hawaii, pineapple juice flowed as easily as water from the kitchen faucet. I remember I just could not get enough of that delicious tropical juice. It was wonderful. Perhaps it was pineapple juice and the surf that helped me overcome my initial longing for our Phoenix home and my girlfriend.

Freezing in Hawaii

I remember our first night in Hawaii. As the sun went down and with a slight wind blowing across the water, we began to get a little chilly. The temperature must have plunged into the low 70s. You've got to remember that we were a family who had just left Phoenix on a June day that was probably 112 degrees. There were sheets on the cots that came with our beach house, but no blankets. My dad admitted that he did not realize we would need blankets and had forgotten to arrange for these. There were no blankets in our baggage and the cargo ship carrying our household belongings wouldn't arrive in Hilo for a couple of weeks.

I remember the 10 of us sitting together in the living room and shivering as if we had just landed in Anchorage, Alaska. Then, there was a knock at the door. We all jumped up and turned toward the living room door. My dad opened the door. There on the front porch were a Hawaiian man and woman. I still remember their brown faces with the widest grins I had ever seen. The man spoke to introduce himself and his wife.

He went on to tell us that he was a member of the Hilo Fire Department. Someone had told him that a haoli (white) family had arrived from the mainland with eight kids and needed to be welcomed to town.

Our new Hawaiian friends came inside to meet the whole family. They shook our hands as they offered their warmest Aloha greeting. The fireman turned to my dad and said, "Mr. Checketts, your kids look a little cold with that ocean breeze blowing. We have brought some blankets from the fire station, if you'd like to use them." That night, we had blankets and we felt welcome in our new Hawaiian home.

An Island on the Island

As time passed, we moved from the leased home to a wonderful home of our own on an island on the island. The Wailuku River flowed down from the high mountains in the center of the island and out to Hilo Bay. In the middle of the river where it ran through the City of Hilo, there was a small island named Reed's Island. That's where my family lived for some time. I came and went during my college years. It was an amazing home with a beautiful lanai (great room/patio) that opened onto a large swimming pool. There were tropical fruit trees of many kinds growing naturally in the yard.

If I remember correctly, there were five families who lived on Reed's Island. These were the Checketts family and four Japanese-Hawaiian families. This was an interesting neighborhood, both geographically and culturally. As I was not a permanent resident on Reed's Island, I had to learn of some of my family's

161

experiences second-hand, but I remember two things about the Japanese-Hawaiian people of Hilo, Hawaii. First of all, at school, their children represented very stiff academic competition for my brothers and sisters. These children and their families set the bar for scholastic achievement very high. The second thing I remember about our Japanese-Hawaiian neighbors was how my parents would speak of them as the absolute most kind and generous neighbors they had ever had.

A Rainbow to Share

We came to love and to admire the Hawaiian and the Japanese people of Hilo, including their special traditions and lifestyles. At one point, after living in the islands for several years, my father developed serious stomach ulcers and had to have a portion of his stomach and his small intestine removed. He relayed this important story to me.

As they were preparing my father for surgery, the doctor approached him and said, "We will have to give you a sizeable transfusion of blood. Unless your family can donate the blood, the blood will come from our local blood bank and represent the multiracial people of Hawaii. Is this okay?" My father's answer was, "Absolutely, I love these islands, and this way I can become 'part Hawaiian.'" My father eventually wrote his autobiography, and he entitled it, "A Rainbow to Share." He explained the title to me as a tribute to the people of Hawaii whose cultures were as diverse as the colors of the rainbow and who had willingly shared their blood with him.

With the idea of ethnic diversity in mind, consider the rainbow. A monochromatic rainbow would not be as beautiful as one composed of many colors. It has been my experience when meeting people from around the globe in 25 countries on five continents that my first commitment needs to be "to reserve judgment." I learned that once I had dined with those of other cultures, watched their traditional dances, listened to their histories, and visited their homes, I would become fascinated, and my respect for their cultures would expand. I discovered that making new cultural acquaintances would bring me a feeling of being broadened, enriched, and often humbled. Humbled in that I realized these things about people of other cultures:

1. **Common Objectives.** Their foremost worries and objectives were similar to mine: finding my purpose, getting ahead, providing for my family, and feeling good about my day.

2. **Their Struggles.** Many other peoples of the world struggle harder to make a living than I do and enjoy far fewer day-to-day conveniences than I do. When I travel to Japan, I realize how very spacious my house is. When I travel to Africa, I realize how wasteful it is to water our lawns with potable water. I remember having one of my friends visit us from Nigeria. He was shocked to see my children dancing in the sprinkler on our lawn and drinking water from the hose.

163

3. **Historical Background for What They Do.** Their cultural histories usually span many centuries, not just a couple hundred years. These histories explain many things about them of which I have been mostly ignorant. Once I have begun to glimpse the significance of their histories, I have experienced many "ahas" about why they believe and act as they do; dress as they do; eat what they eat; and so on. For example, it took me a long time to understand why the English eat the cow's tongue and stomach lining (tripe). I came to realize that if you or I had lived in medieval England and been among the poor and the often hungry serfs who lived in small villages outside the castle, we would not waste any edible part of a cow that we were allowed to keep. As the nobles got all the really yummy cow parts (T-bone steaks, rib-eye steaks, ground-round hamburger patties, and so on.), we would have become creative about making do with the less appetizing bits and pieces that were left over.

4. **Historical Contributions to Us All.** In these fascinating other cultures, I would usually find that one or more of their historical figures had directly or indirectly contributed something vital to the modern quality of life I experience. A perfect example is Ts'ai Lun and his invention of paper.

5. **Food and Dance.** Much of the food of these other cultures is, in fact, colorful and delicious.

164

The traditional dances of other cultures are amazing. I have become spellbound as I have watched the traditional dances of India, for instance.

6. **Craftsmanship and Beauty.** The traditional clothing of people from around the world is often more imaginative, colorful, and functional than the clothing I wear. My son shows us pictures of the Quechuan people of Ecuador and I am awed by the beauty of their hand-woven garments that also protect them from the Andean winds.

The bottom line is that other world cultures are downright fascinating, if you let them be, and if you can see the beauty in opposites. It is amazing to me how many of my neighbors in the United States of America have artifacts from all around the world decorating their homes. Sometimes the cultures thus represented are little understood and even resented by my fellow Americans, and yet the cultural artifacts are nevertheless cherished as household ornaments.

Religions of the World

What an important part religion plays in our cultures. It is a major element of our cultural diversity. We would like to believe that here is a great future opportunity for the coming together of religious philosophies and traditions.

I am a Christian. Without sounding as though I am patronizing those of other faiths, I wish to express how intrigued I am by the beliefs of others. I recall staying in the Raffles Hotel in Singapore a few years ago. I was very far from home, had been on the road for a couple of weeks, and was feeling lonely and bored. As I lay on my bed contemplating my situation, I rolled over toward the nightstand and opened the top drawer to see what might be there to read. I probably expected to find a *Gideon Bible*. Instead, I found the *Teachings of Buddha*. I had never read these before, so I browsed the pages. One paragraph caught my eye, and I proceeded to read. I discovered the most reverent, awe-inspiring, protective, uplifting, informative description of the beautiful things that surround us in nature: birds, flowers, insects, animals of all kinds, fruit trees, and more. Anyone who read these things would want to grab some binoculars and go bird watching or call the hotel concierge to order a vase of fresh-cut flowers for his hotel room, which I then noticed was already sitting there on my hotel credenza. Buddha's teachings made me think twice before I squished the next beetle I saw struggling to make its way along the sidewalk on the busy Singapore streets. Thank you, most venerable Buddha, for your teachings.

As I have traveled through Muslim countries in the Persian Gulf region and in West Africa, I have been blessed to meet those who were intrigued with our religious differences and who chose not to provoke arguments or promote resentment among us. I learned how blessed it is to be called Alhaji or "pilgrim." I came to appreciate, even more, the history of Father Abraham, which I had been taught as a boy. I know times have changed since 9/11 and since I was there among my Muslim friends. How sad I am for what has been damaged by those who take any religious belief to its extremes of intolerance. Though our religions may divide us, our faith should unite us.

Nationalism

There are those in the United States who think Canadians are foreigners. Well, maybe they are in one sense. They are also our North American brothers and sisters as are the people of Mexico. This makes me recall a meeting in Frankfurt, Germany, a number of years ago. A diverse group of international business professionals was gathered. Around our conference table were those familiar placards with the names of those individuals who would be participating in the meeting. Several of us began to take note of the distinctive cultural origins of the surnames we saw. The German names stood out. These were long and somewhat difficult to pronounce, or so we Anglo "foreigners" thought. The English names were shorter and easier to pronounce, or so we of Anglo origin believed. Then there were French names and Italian names and Greek names and some even more exotic names from various parts of Eastern Europe. I found the Indian names fascinating as they usually had some special meaning beyond the name itself. Most of us knew that the Scandinavian names usually signified family connections, as in "Ericson."

As we commented on the colorful and interesting names, someone turned to me and asked, "Darby, what would be a typical American name?" I stopped and thought. Then, it dawned on me that the typical American names I knew from my travels through New Jersey, South Carolina, Texas, Wisconsin, California, New Mexico, Louisiana, and a total of 47 of our 50 states were the same as the German, Scandinavian, Italian, French, Indian, and other names represented on the placards right there on our conference table. To the question about typical American names I replied, "There is no typical American name. We are a melting pot of all the cultures represented around this table." The only typical American name might be that of a Native American such as Sakagawea or Geronimo, and that's a whole other story.

The message here is for my fellow Americans. When we discredit other cultures of the world, we discredit our own. This is analogous to someone saying they like the rich flavor of a vegetable stew as they criticize the weird shapes and colors of the vegetables in it. "I'm a potato and I don't like carrots in my stew." It's only through the blending of flavors that a stew becomes so delicious. Such is the intrigue of a melting pot of cultural backgrounds and traditions. Someone remarked the other day that their favorite American food was Mexican food. That is an intriguing comment.

Corporate Culture

We live with cultural differences every day—differences that are, in fact, tied to our places of work. Do you think someone from Burlington Northern Railways might have a few challenging months as they began a new job with Apple Computer? How about somebody moving from Frito Lay to Citibank or from the Bureau of Lands and Mines to Starbucks? Corporations are keepers of their own culture—rightly so. In fact, any consultant who would help a company build brand loyalty would talk about being distinctive and about differentiating your company from other companies, even those within the same industry. It is the difference that is powerful. Ask Apple. For years, their slogan was: "Think Different." All of these differences make for a competitive and yet vibrant economy with an array of businesses that can meet the diverse needs of a multicultural country such as the United States of America.

In building a great company, those who lead it seek to strengthen their own unique "corporate culture." At the same time, they would be well advised to not become steeped in their particular industry culture to the point that they could not easily assimilate someone from Burlington Northern or Frito Lay. In fact a "Frito Lay" foreigner would be a good "flavoring" for the ever more breakthrough culture at Burlington Northern. And a Burlington Northern employee would bring much "on time" discipline to help Starbucks customers get that hot "cuppa" in a timely manner.

Communities and Neighborhoods

I've never lived in any of the boroughs of New York City, but I've visited every one. Are you from Brooklyn, the Bronx, Staten Island, Queens, or Manhattan? My, oh my, what an incredible difference there is from neighborhood to neighborhood. What a marvelous mix of humanity. There are few better places to eat and be entertained on this Earth than in greater

New York City. I wonder why. As I wrote this book, I primarily resided in Mesa, Arizona. To the north and west of Mesa lies Scottsdale. In a drive of just 10 miles, we can sense the difference. My wife Sharon and I are glad we live in Mesa but we are also glad we can *go out to eat* in Scottsdale. I may complain that they're all rich and uppity over there, but I know it's not true. I'm just jealous. And I know they're good people, too. But, what's most important is that they've got art galleries and restaurants to live for.

As I prepared for this chapter on cultural opposites, I happened to have just read a U.S. *News & World Report* issue with these two articles: "Culture Clash in Denmark" and "Capitalism That Crosses Cultures." This latter article talks about a financial services and investment company, Shariah Capital of New Canaan, Connecticut, which is helping American companies qualify for investment by members of the Muslim business community who are looking for investment products that comply with *Sharia* (Islamic law as laid out in the Koran). Helping Muslims find suitable places to invest their petrodollars to help American companies is an excellent example of turning opposition into innovation.

Of further interest is the cultural insight this article provides: "*Sharia* strictly forbids Muslims from taking or charging interest, and holds that money should be lent only on physical assets. It bars speculation and prohibits investing in items like pork, alcohol, gambling, and pornography." For Americans with too much high-interest debt, who should perhaps avoid speculation and gambling, and who may choose to eat less pork, drink less alcohol, and steer clear of pornography; these may be helpful guidelines. My folks taught me that the truth is the truth, no matter where it originates. I am a Christian and a moderate capitalist and yet I can learn from and respect the principles of Sharia. I do not have to fully embrace a philosophy to appreciate it. I would hope that the Muslims I meet would respond in a similar fashion to the principles I have found to be helpful.

We are living in an age when certain culture clashes have come to the surface with sad and frightening implications. And yet, as we look back in history, there were conquering hordes that rode into foreign lands, unleashed great violence, spoiled villages, and took others captive. Culture clashes are nothing new. In fact, the culture clashes of the 21st century are far less violent and disruptive than at most times in history. The problem is the world has shrunk and we now have a "global village." Many of us have envisioned, perhaps naïvely and prematurely, that the time has come when all of us on the planet might realize that we can peacefully coexist and enjoy the rich diversity of our world without so much intolerance. We can bring an end to the poverty that breeds so much discontent and thereby bring an end to the war. Is this a naïve vision? Perhaps the most important book of our time, written by Jeffrey Sachs, is *The End of Poverty*. He would tell us that such a vision is not naïve; it is simply a test of our collective will. Are there any answers? Perhaps there are no absolute answers, but there are questions worth asking and ideas worth sharing. There is a great deal at stake in this first decade of a new millennium. Our global cultural conflicts are humanity's greatest opportunity to transform opposition into innovation.

Who Owns the World?

Many lay claim to the world's real estate. However, considering the world as a whole, from its molten core to its atmosphere, from its oceans and valleys to its lofty mountaintops, from its glorious tropical gardens and marvelous animal life to its diverse human inhabitants, there appear to be three most plausible answers to the question of *who owns the world....*

o **Someone or some group or nation does.**
   Perhaps there are those still sufficiently arrogant and politically ambitious to presume that "we must dominate the world."

• **God does.** Most of the world's inhabitants profess faith in a higher power or a supernatural *life force* operating in the universe. Such a higher power would have a respectable claim upon the world.

o **All of us do.** The most plausible claim would be, practically speaking, that the collective members of the human family *own* this world. If God is the landlord, then we may be viewed as tenants with a lease-purchase option.

We Are in This Together

We do experience a shrinking world where access to each other is quicker and easier than ever before. To view our planet as a global village is not merely a poetic ideal, but an ecological, economic, and social reality. For all of the years humankind has lived upon the Earth, it is reasonable to expect that we are living in our most enlightened age. And yet, we still operate at a level of tribalism that shows us to be ever suspicious of those *others* on the planet who *do not look as we do, dress as we do, speak as we do, think as we do,* or *worship as we do.* We are still prone to anger, to disrespect, to taking advantage, and to resorting to war. Is it time for *true enlightenment* to take hold? If we each seek prosperity, happiness, and our own spiritual fulfillment, will it come more easily in a world that is unified in striving for peace? What principles can guide us? Perhaps, as the citizens of a global community, we can moderate our potential for conflict and agree that:

1. **Each of us has a stake and needs a voice.** Together, as the human family, we all *own* this world. In the ultimate spirit of democracy, each member of this family has a stake in how the world's resources are utilized. We each need a voice in how the world's institutions function to serve us.

2. **Together, we are stewards of the planet.** We will prosper more fully as we protect the air we breathe, the oceans, the gardens, the animal life, and each other. We must share our discoveries and our technologies for the betterment of the human condition where there is now poverty, disease, and suffering.

173

3. **We must respect and protect.** Protecting each
   other takes these basic forms: (a) to do no harm;
   (b) to guarantee freedom from oppression; (c) to
   respect individual beliefs, values, and traditions
   insofar as these do not threaten the safety and
   well-being of others; and (d) to provide evermore
   equal opportunities for good health, education,
   and economic security, *accompanied by a commitment
   to individual responsibility and effort.*

4. **Global commerce benefits us all.** From the days
   of shopping in the village bazaar to today's commerce in a global village, we have always been
   economically interdependent. As we look with
   hope to a post-Iraqi War era, any lingering resentment and hatred, any international recriminations,
   any ancient rivalries, and any lopsided political
   ambitions are nothing but shortsighted and damaging to us all. Even the human family can "get
   over it" and move on.

5. **We are unified against terrorism.** The most serious disruption to our human family has become
   the fear of and the acts of terrorism. Terrorism
   thrives on hatred, the lowest and most despicable
   of human emotions. It grows from ugly prejudice
   and suspicion. It so swiftly threatens the prosperity of all. We must unite to eradicate it.

6. **The need for war is a sign of failure.** In the
   post 9/11 era, we can conclude that warfare may

174

sometimes be necessary to defend the freedom of nations or to correct the injustices that people may suffer. However, it should be the great hope of all humankind that warfare will be increasingly unnecessary in an increasingly enlightened world. Otherwise, war is a sign of our failure to overcome the most unpleasant of human attributes: selfishness, greed, dishonesty, deception, and violence. Most of all, it is a sign of our failure to communicate. It is the most damaging form of human conflict, which we must overcome. We must demonstrate that our civilizations have advanced sufficiently that we can find ways to resolve our deepest differences in ways that do not destroy the very family and village of which we are all a part.

7. **Children are our number-one priority.** The greatest priority for our human family is the safety, education, and happiness of our CHILDREN. All other preoccupations are trivial by comparison. As humankind marches toward each fateful decision, our path will be determined or altered by these simple questions: "What is best for our children? What will our children learn from our actions? Will the world be a safer, friendlier, and more stimulating place in which to grow up and to prosper?" Here is where we will find the common ground we most need to find. Here is where we will transform opposition into innovation with the most lasting benefit to us all.

175

The Great Age

We talk of the various "ages of humanity," including the *Industrial Age* that leveraged the human body with machinery of all kinds…the *Information Age* that leveraged the human mind with computer and communication technologies. With the beginning of this new millennium, we have entered a new age, which we have yet to name. If we have leveraged the human body and the human mind, perhaps this is the age wherein we will leverage the human spirit. *What spirit is this?* It is the *spirit of unity* that transcends all immediate conflicts to find solutions amidst the diversity of our amazing world. Buddha would teach us all—Christians, Muslims, Jews, Hindus, Buddhists, and those of all other faiths and cultures—to "tread lightly where living things grow." It is the *spirit of reverence* for every thing and every creature that exists here on Earth for some purpose—a purpose we should seek more to understand and less to debate.

Special Invitation: May I invite you to visit my Website at *www.DarbyChecketts.com* to request a complimentary copy of the e-book, "Who Owns the World: The Parable of Tehya." **The Parable of Tehya** is set in a time long ago that seems like yesterday. It takes place in a faraway land that may remind you of a village nearby. The parable reveals ancient wisdom that is truth for a modern world. It is about *original beauty* and *tribes* and *the importance of one child.* The images in the story are a composite of wonderful things I have learned through the years, beautiful places in the 25 countries I have visited, and my impressions of marvelous people of both the past and the present in many cultures around the world. In the book, Tehya asks her father the profound question: **Who owns the world?** At the conclusion of the book, Tehya's mother reveals to the great chiefs what is most important for our extended world family at this time in history.

Chapter 11
The Power of
Ideological Opposites

I often teach about the "Five Arenas of Life."

Family / Friends	Community	Career / Business	Self	Other _____

I invite those in my seminar audiences to consider the first four arenas as those we nearly all have in common and then to add a fifth arena of their choosing, such as a spiritual commitment (religious affiliation), a cherished hobby, an avid sports interest, a key financial investment, a book writing project, and so on. I point out that life is sort of a juggling act wherein we all try to find the right life balance. Next, I ask the group to rank the five arenas to identify which is of number-one importance and which arenas are of lesser importance. There is quite a debate that follows. There are those who immediately state the importance of the family as the basic building block of society and the principal support group we all need. Someone

177

else will then point out that, if you do not cultivate a successful career, your self-esteem will suffer and you will be unable to provide for your family. Then, those who are especially committed to physical health and emotional well-being speak up for the "self." Their argument is like those instructions we are given on airplanes to "put on your own oxygen mask first, before you try to help others."

The "ideological" debate continues. Ultimately, I turn to the group and say, "I am going to be bold enough to presume to tell you which of these arenas is truly number one. It is 'Family and Friends.' It is 'Community' and 'Career/Business' and 'Self' and that important 'Other' category of yours." I explain the great fallacy of trading off the major arenas of life against each other. This is the most unfortunate example of the "tyranny of the *or*." The truth is: we will only thrive as we strive for a level of excellence in all five arenas. Suppose you tried to convince your boss that you could only be a second-rate engineer because you needed to be a top-notch father. Imagine trying to convince your spouse that because your boss expected you to be the best possible engineer, you could not be a truly first-rate father to your children. Here is where we must all find the "genius of the *and*" instead of the "tyranny of the *or*." When someone asks how can you juggle all five arenas and be excellent in all of them, you can reply, "Yes, I will." Remember the optimist's answer to everything. It means you are not exactly sure of the answer, but you know you must somehow reconcile the demands of the five arenas. And, actually, there is a very pragmatic answer to the situational

178

dilemmas and ideological dichotomies that these five arenas represent. The answer is simply to prioritize all the "stuff" that you think you must do in each individual arena. The problems with the five arenas are mostly tied to the long to-do lists that follow underneath each of the five headings. We come to believe we must be *all* things and do *all* things in *all* five arenas, when we must simply *do the thing that counts most right now* as we happen to be in whatever arena we're *in*. My simple philosophy is: *wherever you are; be there!* It's about *now*. It's about the moment. It's about the fact that you can only be in one place, doing one thing especially well at a given time, so choose the place carefully and focus all of your attention on the opportunity at hand in the present moment.

The previous father/engineer scenario provides the opportunity for a reflective exercise in life planning and time management. It is also an opportunity to fine-tune your philosophy for dealing with the ideological conflicts that occur as you interact with others who share the Five Arenas of Life with you. Next time somebody comes up to you with that particular tone of voice and says, "You know, your family is the most important thing in life," *reserve judgment.* You may be thinking to yourself, "Oh great, here's one of those 'family is paramount' fanatics trying to give me a guilt trip because I work such long hours." Instead of arguing the relative importance of family or family values, say this: "You are right, family is so important. When I am with my family, I really work at letting them know how precious they are to me. I ask myself what they most need from me to strengthen the love we have for each other.

And, I work at focusing my energies in order to really be present with them." Such a conversation is an opportunity to experience the power of being agreeable. *Being agreeable* doesn't mean you have to *totally agree* and "give in" to someone else's point of view. Instead, you quickly recognize that ideological dichotomies are usually reconcilable. You see the opportunity to transform opposition into innovation.

Absolutes

We could list a myriad of philosophies people have about their five arenas, which result in the disagreements and the arguments we periodically have with each other. One thing we humans are prone to doing is taking positions in the "absolute" that aren't absolute. It was my great mentor, John Arnold, who would teach his clients so eloquently the importance of learning to deal with interests, not positions. As we discussed earlier, positions are *alternative outcomes* in terms of how a problem might be solved or, more generally, how we come to believe life *should be.* Our underlying interests help us select or create the outcomes that would ultimately be in our "best interests" overall. Among these interests, there may be some that are *absolute requirements* and others that are *highly desirable.* Many arguments can be prevented by realizing that there are fewer "absolutes" than we may think. Let me illustrate by going back to the importance of family. Consider two positions....

Position #1: Your family is a top priority and you need to spend more time with them.

Position #2: My family is a top priority and I need to make my time with them count.

Which of these is true? Is Position #1 absolutely true? If so, can you or I prove it? Can I prove that *you* need to spend more time with your family? If the answer to any of these questions is no, then your needing to spend more time with your family is not an *absolute requirement* and I would be doing you a great disservice to let my position on family life turn into one of those famous "guilt trips" that we seem to like to create for ourselves and others.

Here is a different question: Is it *highly desirable* to spend more time with your family, if you possibly can? Most of us would probably say yes. This latter line of reasoning takes so much pressure off our ideological debate over the importance of family. Now, the discussion can turn to either: (a) how to find more time to spend with your family or (b) if it is not going to be easy to spend *more* time with them, how can you make the time you do spend *more meaningful* and more memorable. Aha! We have just transformed ideological opposition into innovation. A *debate* over the importance of family has now transformed into a *discussion* about making family interactions as frequent and as meaningful as possible.

In a somewhat more scientific context, something that is truly an *absolute requirement* must be measurable either in terms of a maximum allocation of resources or a minimum standard of performance. For example, if one of your work team members were to take the budgetary position, "We absolutely cannot

181

spend any more money on this project," I would hope you would be allowed to ask, "How much is more?" If your associate said, "Not more than $250,000," the next question needs to be: "What if we happen to need $255,000, will you shut the project down?" If the answer is, "No, of course not," then *not* spending more money is *not* an absolute requirement. It is apparently *highly desirable* that you all work together to stay as close to $250,000 as possible. Do you see how this insight can help to defuse debates over the budget?

On the other hand, if someone says, "We must have zero defects as a result of our manufacturing operation," you may ask, "Does this mean that a single defect will shut down the operation, or is there some minimum standard of performance that we can accept?" They may reply, "These turbine blades are the heart of the jet engines we manufacture for Army helicopters and there is zero tolerance for error. If there is any detectible defect in a single blade, you must push one of the red buttons on the assembly line and shut the entire operation down immediately." Now, that sounds like an absolute requirement.

Choose your battles. Many "absolutes" should be subject to open discussion and a few will not be. The secret is to not create absolutes where there are none. Otherwise, you may go to battle, create conflict, and put your reputation, your relationships, or even your life on the line when the justification is not there. Instead, more discussion, some negotiation, and the willingness to compromise would be advisable before you draw that line in the sand and dare someone to cross it.

Back to family values: "You must spend more time with your family." How much is more? And what will happen if I don't? Will my children disappear in a puff of smoke? You see, spending more time with your family cannot be an *absolute requirement*. It is a *highly desirable* objective. So, next time you are tempted to tell your parenting partner that she or he must spend more time with the kids, please reconsider. Save the argument. Instead, suggest that "Johnnie" is struggling with his math homework and would really benefit from a little extra help sometime this evening.

From time to time, we all take positions that we presume to be absolute. To be "absolute," these would need to be based on underlying interests that are non-negotiable and yet seldom are. Are there absolutes in life and in business? Absolutely! I could now turn this chapter into an extremely controversial discussion of "What are life's absolutes?" I won't. However, this question may be a subject worthy of personal contemplation and thoughtful discussion among those you love most or those who depend upon you to serve them in your daily work and in your community activities. At some point, there may be guiding principles for which we stand, true and that we would like others to not tread upon as important elements of "who we are." It is important to know what you, your significant others, your workmates, and your neighbors choose to "stand for" with some considerable degree of reverence and resoluteness.

Let's take the time to acknowledge where our ideological opposites typically show up. One interesting category of ideological opposites is "those that result in 'guilt trips.'"

We will define a *guilt trip* as "the guilty feeling that results when someone says or implies something that makes you or me feel *not okay* or somehow put down." Another category would be those self-righteous proclamations of "I know the truth and you don't." We'll call these "having a corner on the truth." These can result in religious rivalry, nasty political partisanship, and highly disruptive workplace conflicts.

Guilt Trips

As you contemplate the following statements, ask yourself if each one of them is truly an "absolute" or rather indicative of an opportunity to discuss underlying interests and find the common ground that will transform opposition into innovation.

1. Children always need to be in bed before midnight.
2. If you flirt with someone else at the office, you are unfaithful to me.
3. Americans must save more money.
4. French fries and other fried foods are destroying the health of people around the world.
5. You should always pay cash for a car and avoid borrowing money.
6. You watch too much TV.
7. The best thing you can do is to pay off your home mortgage as soon as possible.

8. You should stop doodling and pay attention to me.

9. If you don't start exercising, you'll get diabetes.

10. To really keep your mind sharp, you need to read two or three books a month.

11. If you can't even remember our anniversary, you must not love me.

12. Green and orange are the two worst colors you could possibly wear together.

I hope you have some fun considering these. Take the last one. Can this become the basis for serious ideological conflict? Yes, folks have big debates about which are the best colors to wear, given your complexion and other factors. This can go so far as to create a debate over which is the true "power tie" to wear to a board of directors meeting. My position is: Never, ever wear brown—absolutely not—unless you work for UPS, of course. I'm just kidding about brown. You make your own decision about this rich earth tone. One of my favorite ties is mostly brown.

We will now examine a category of opposites that can contribute to religious bigotry, political mudslinging, and declining morale in the workplace. It is the category that deals with our interpretations of "what is truth" and who can make a claim to have a corner on the truth. Is it reasonable to think that some do possess more truth than others? Yes, I think so. Does such special access to truth give them the license to dictate to the consciences of others? The answer may be *not*

185

necessarily or *it depends*. Do others who possess such truth have a responsibility to share what they know? Yes, if it is likely to help those who would listen. Is it important how they share it? Yes, and here we contrast those who would be our teachers versus those who would become dictators. There is a fine line between zeal and bigotry.

A Corner on the Truth: Religion

I will admit to you that, in the entire book, the next couple of paragraphs were the most challenging paragraphs for me to write. For starters, I believe in separation of church and state. I also believe that it is my responsibility, in a book such as this, to not get on my soap box, and yet to be truthful. I must be willing to examine my own views in light of the opposing viewpoints so that you can see me wrestle with the need and the opportunity to find common ground for our understanding. For example, in the previous chapter, I openly shared my views about "who owns the world." These views have some merit, but may not take into account all the political realities of life in our highly complex global village. Nevertheless, I would hope that I could join the worldwide discussion as we all work to make the planet a safer, friendlier, and more peaceful place.

What is difficult for me is this subject of religion. Why? The subject is so personal, and it is perhaps the only one that transcends what we know for a fact about this world to also include a consideration of the things we accept on faith. What we may call absolutes in a religious context are principles we have been taught to believe in, often as "eternal truths" that we accept as beyond our complete understanding as humans. And here's my dichotomy. It is my *grand* dichotomy: On one hand, I believe in God and that God is not wishy-washy. On the other hand, I certainly do not want to alienate you with a discussion of what you may consider to be religious dogma. If you will allow me to create the basis for some reflection and conversation, I will be most grateful.

I believe there are principles that make the universe operate as it does for good reasons. For example, if we were to explore absolutes, we might agree that, in this world, gravity is an absolute. God probably determined that gravity should not periodically turn on and then turn off again. If it did, many of the things we humans try to do each day would become especially difficult to do on any consistent basis, and some of us would periodically float off the planet and into space. Imagine if gravity were situational and selective—that sometimes some people experienced more gravity than others. Quite frankly, I am grateful that gravity is an absolute. I do not fully understand it. Let's not debate it. Let's accept the truth of it.

Now, already we could have a debate about the absolute existence of God. Did God put gravity in operation, or is gravity the serendipitous and convenient result of objects revolving and rotating around each other in space? If we seriously engaged in such a debate, I confess that I might fail to listen to those who do not believe as I do. I must remind myself to find the truth in whatever others may believe.

187

I view the search for truth as similar to assembling a great intergalactic puzzle, one that we are each trying to piece together in our own individual way. We find a piece of the puzzle here and another piece there. Some of our wisest teachers possess a collection of the puzzle pieces and are especially helpful in accelerating our discovery of the truth. What is important is to not diminish someone else's collection of puzzle pieces, for these may somehow fit together with yours and mine to assist us in creating a more complete picture. Thus, we may question whether any one person or group has a corner on the truth. Instead, we will come to acknowledge some universal body of truth that we all seek. We will be thankful that others on the planet are willing to share their fascinating puzzle pieces with us. Then our faith can unite us rather than divide us.

If you asked me for an "absolute" in all of religion, I would respond that my sense is that religion is about love—about acknowledging God's love for us all as we love one another. This love is manifest as we serve each other and resist the inclination to debate our religious tenets. Instead, we choose to reserve judgment and to share the truths we know in a spirit of love. We allow each person their free agency.

One more footnote is this: debating the existence of God is, for many, a mere intellectual exercise, for the answer is unknowable in the absolute. Though there are signs that point to an intelligent force at work in the universe, the ultimate conclusions we may reach about such a force must be based on faith. And now we come full circle as to why this is such a sensitive and challenging subject for me. Whether you and I believe in God or not, we cannot totally discount that there are certain mysteries in the universe around us that make us wonder at it all. What does it mean to wonder? Is it to ask ourselves, "So, what is 'out there'?" Is it to conclude that we are really not certain and yet to acknowledge that the wonder whispers to us of something grand? Would we be wise to keep our options (our positions) open rather than to become too dogmatic in the name of religion? If there is something grand in store, we should prepare ourselves for it and help others along the way. Perhaps it would be best to cultivate the curiosity of a child—to just enjoy the wonder of it all and to allow others the same privilege.

A Corner on the Truth: Politics

Those who have observed American politics in recent years have heard us talk of *blue states* and *red states* when, deep down, we know that we are better as a nation as we strive to be the *United* States.

In recent years, Americans have seen their leaders and themselves more ideologically and philosophically divided than at any other time in recent history. We see politicians standing or sitting (or refusing to stand) on their two separate sides of the General Assembly Hall. We are thankful that there is opportunity for opposing views on the issues and that our Constitution allows us the freedom of dissent. At the same time, once the discussion is over, there must be a coming together for the common good. We'd like to cry out against special interests, corruption, stalemates, filibusters, and lobbying. We would like to say that the underlying interests of the American people are life, liberty, and the pursuit of happiness. The extension of these values is our collective desire for public safety, shared economic opportunity, and a solid education for our children. When will our special interests give way to our common interests? When will jockeying for position give way to doing what is right? When will a spirit of confrontation give way to a spirit of diplomacy? If ever there was a *grand* opportunity to transform opposition into innovation it is NOW in this great nation of ours and in a world that is too easily torn apart by ideological conflict.

Can we change? Of course we can. How fast can any of us change our ways? The answer: Instantly. If I asked you to stop driving your car so fast, you could change *now*. If I asked you to stop watching so much TV, you could turn it off now. The challenge would be to turn your new situational behavior change into a lasting habit. If people are engaged in an argumentative discussion, how quickly can they stop the conversation? The answer: Immediately. If I am arguing with you, I can decide that it isn't worth it. I can decide that the negative interaction is hurting me as much as you. I can walk away. I may still be angry, but I have stopped the argument. I can decide that there are more important things than winning the argument. And, if we stop arguing, can we get over it? People are getting over stuff every day and moving on. Can politicians get over it and move on? How quickly? The answers are: Yes, and Now. How would this work? They would learn to deal with interests rather than take "absolute" positions on the

190

issues. This is true where our domestic affairs are concerned, and our international affairs as well. Why should politicians consider something so idealistic in the midst of the stark realities they now face? The answer: Because the stakes are so high and because our grandchildren are waiting for their opportunity to inherit a beautiful and a peaceful planet. There, I've said it. Thanks for letting me. Now, let's discuss it further.

So, what about Democrats and Republicans—about blue states and red states—and about the wars that rage? Should there be no war, or is war a fact of life? The answer is the optimist's answer: Yes, there should be no war and, yes, war is a fact of life. Where is the innovation in these opposite views? We can deplore war as we stand ready to defend ourselves. We will view war as our last resort. We can stand ready to defend ourselves and yet project our goodwill before we rattle our swords. And, war will not become a "plank" in anybody's political platform. It comes down to two groups of politicians who are all our national leaders looking at both sides of an argument to come up with a solution that does transcend partisanship and will prove to be what is best for our children and all children around the world.

Should we have big government or little government? The answer: We should have enough government to do what government needs to do most. Thus, the debate in the halls of government should not be over the size of government, but the *purposes* of government. Should we have more taxes or more tax cuts? The debate should not be about taxes, but about what *revenue* the government needs to do its job, and how to

191

find the most equitable and efficient way to get that revenue, to keep track of it, and to put it to great use to benefit our citizens and not waste it.

When we let the issues polarize us and then label each political party with its particular positions on the issues, the power of opposites is lost. We are blessed to live in a nation where debating the issues is allowed so that we see the issues from differing perspectives. Then, we can identify what is the greater good—irrespective of political parties—that will serve the best interests of our nation as a whole. Is this an idealistic notion? Yes.

What is your position on idealism? Mine is this: without our ideals, we lower our standards to accept whatever we perceive to be "human nature." Whatever "human nature" may be, it is too easy an excuse for not becoming all that we can become. What is the opposing position on "idealism"? I have been told that we should not deal in platitudes, and I agree. What are platitudes? These are trite remarks. What are trite remarks? These are remarks that are "made stale and uninteresting by repeated use." So, the final question would be: which of our ideals are stale and uninteresting, and why have these become so? Is it because we have thrown up our hands and said, "That won't work; it goes against human nature"? In the world of politics, it is too easy to retreat to the idea of blue states and red states as we unknowingly turn our backs on the ideals of the United States of America for which we stand. We can move beyond the dichotomy of which party is right to what can the two parties do to unite us? That would be opposition transformed into innovation on a grand scale that the world could admire.

A Corner on the Truth: Workplace

Have you ever worked for an ogre? Reserve judgment. He may be a Shrek in disguise. To discuss workplace disagreements and conflicts, we would have to admit that there are overly authoritarian bosses—and unduly stubborn employees as well. And just how many absolutes are there in business? Not as many as we think. Employee safety and customer satisfaction are good candidates for "absolute" status. Corporate ethics, obeying the law, and honoring the public trust are candidates in most companies. Other than these, most of what happens in business is "highly desirable" or perhaps "not that highly desirable, but nice to have." The bottom line is that there are enough dictators out there without the need for excessively authoritarian behavior in the workplace where we each spend most of our lives. Furthermore, the role of team "snoopervisor" has given way to the role of team leader. What about stubborn employees? Take the advice of Jimmy Stewart and "try pleasant." We need to nurture a spirit of openness that says, the truth about how to get along with each other, how to improve our products, how to serve our customers better, and how to reward our stakeholders is to be found in the ideas, opinions, perspectives, and beliefs of each and every member of the team. Let's listen!

What can you do where you work? First of all, share copies of this book. Secondly, contact me (the author) and I'll tell you where to buy my guidebook entitled *29 Questions That Will Energize Your Team*. Address those particular questions your team most needs to answer in order to turn up the respect and the energy so that you can transform your conflicts into opportunities. The essence of the book is conveyed by that key principle we have discussed multiple times: "Great teams learn to talk about what they may *need to* talk about *before* they *have to* talk about it." The repetition of this principle is very deliberate. Here is another jump start on your Principles of Team Conduct. You can use the *29 Questions* guidebook to help you list the situations you need to constructively confront, or you can simply brainstorm a list of these and reach agreement on how you will handle each situation. Here are further examples to assist you (next page):

Difficult/Challenging Situations	Principles of Team Conduct
1. When problems arise, there is a tendency to want to "pin the blame" on something or somebody. This is the "sell out" scenario.	1. **Deal with issues, not personalities.** Remember to fix the problem, not the blame.
2. When people state strong opinions, there's a tendency to overreact and become defensive.	2. **Reserve Judgment.** Before taking sides on the issues, let's be sure we understand the issues.
3. The customer seems overly distraught and impatient. The tendency is to want to move on and *gloss over* underlying issues.	3. **Listen with the ears of a detective and the heart of a friend.** Listen for the *facts and* the *impacts.* Ask the customer to help you understand why he or she feels so strongly.
4. Natural rivalries often exist among team members and among departments within an organization.	4. **Instead of EGO, how about WE-GO?**
5. There is a tendency to hurry and forget to keep others informed—to not "close the loop," as they say.	5. **TTB: Touch the Bases!** Take a lesson from the game of baseball. You can run around the ball diamond to home plate, but it doesn't count unless you "touch the bases."
6. [Keep going.]	6. [Make these simple and memorable.]

195

I offer this definition of the spirit of teamwork....

There is no greater human triumph than when a group of people cease their contentions and decide that some purpose deserves the commitment of all. Then comes the pulling together. Teamwork is strength in numbers, creativity through diversity, lots of hard work, and some fun.

Chapter 12
Getting What You Need by Helping Others Succeed

What follows is the TOOL KIT chapter with some tips and techniques you can use in your day-to-day communication and in your overall commitment to transform opposition into innovation. As we have discussed from time to time throughout the book, there are numerous approaches to the subject and the reality of conflict. One approach is to view conflict as a stressful phenomenon that must somehow be handled, minimized, or managed. As you will recall, one extreme philosophy is the emphasis on "winning through intimidation," which is based on shrewdness and your ability to maneuver through situations to get the upper hand. Often, conflict is associated with the need to *negotiate*. Negotiating may suggest some sort of intellectual "wrestling match." Or it can be seen as a helpful process for working out our differences and reaching some compromise in order to get on with life and business. "Negotiation" is actually one of the most fundamental of all human interactions, whether you are negotiating a salary increase with your boss, a Middle East peace accord, or tying to get your mom to fix your favorite dessert for dinner tonight. As we engage in the process in a constructive way, it is our intent to influence others and to win their support.

It is important to examine our individual mindsets concerning the subject of negotiating. Let me ask you, do you see *negotiating* as a situation in which you are concerned that you may be taken advantage of? Do you see it as an interaction requiring principally "salesmanship" so that you can get the outcome you desire? Or, do you see the "win-win" opportunity in negotiating? My view of "negotiating skill" is that it allows you and me to more easily identify the *common ground* so that we can get to the *common good* faster. Once we get past our stated positions and come to understand our respective and underlying interests, it is my experience that we are more likely to discover what we have in common than to discover that we must compete.

Pessimists and optimists debate whether the glass is half empty or half full. Win-lose negotiators versus win-win negotiators debate whether the half-glass in question means "there is only enough for me" or there is a quarter-glass for me and a quarter-glass for you. If I let you drink, there will then be two of us to search for the oasis where we will find the abundance of water that will meet our greater needs. It's about the power of goodwill and generosity. Thus the title of this chapter.

198

Let's examine the process of negotiating and influencing in greater detail. The preceding chapters have helped us understand conflict and to cultivate the mindset that allows us to look for the energy inside it. This chapter presumes that you want to get that energy out and get going. Let's build on the fundamental communication skills we discussed in Chapter 8.

Negotiating/Influencing Styles

Remember Chapter 9 and our discussion of *The Power of Personality Opposites*. Here is a quick review....

	Values	Asks	Needs	Buys	Learns From
Navigator	Accuracy	What?	Time	Price/Value	Documentation
Organizer	Predictability	How?	Clarity	Reliability	Checklists
Facilitator	Relationships	Who?	Participation	Enjoyment	Discussion
Visionary	Freedom	Why?	Space	Performance	Experimentation

The *Navigator*, the *Organizer*, the *Facilitator*, and the *Visionary*.... Each individual with whom you interact will seek the outcomes that are important to her or to him in distinctive ways. They will see situations through their individual lens of concern or opportunity. It is essential that you understand the fundamental dispositions of those with whom you negotiate, whether these individuals happen to be coworkers, bosses, your children, your life partner, salespersons, hospital nurses, schoolteachers, customers, or your next-door neighbors.

To illustrate, suppose you are lying in your hospital bed (heaven forbid) and you are as sick of the institutional food as you are of being sick. A nurse comes to your bed and you ask, "Can I please have a Snickers bar?" She frowns, shakes her finger at you, and says, "You know your doctor wants to keep your sugar intake way down. See this chart on the end of your bed? This shows your blood sugar level, and it is supposed to be at least two points under this red line. Until that happens, no Snickers bar, I'm afraid." Is this a negotiation? Yes. Does this nurse sound like a Navigator, an Organizer, a Facilitator, or a Visionary? Most likely, you have just met a person who is operating from the *Navigator/Organizer* perspective.

Let's try again. Suppose you ask for a Snickers bar and the nurse says, "We'll see. Tell me how long it has been since you had something sweet." You answer, "It must be days." The nurse says, "Let me check with the dietician, okay?" What is the disposition of this new negotiating partner? This nurse is more likely to be approaching your situation with the perspective of a *Facilitator*.

The key here is to be aware enough of where other folks are coming from so you can choose your strategy accordingly. What do you say to the Facilitator nurse? You say, "Thanks, and could you please ask the dietician if I can have even just one of those small Halloween treat-size Snickers?"

You face a greater challenge in winning the support of the chart-toting, red-line watching Navigator/Organizer nurse. Here's the "don't do." It would probably be best to not take this approach: "Come on, Nurse, I'm paying the hospital bill. That's my chart and I want a Snickers bar regardless of what the chart says." Oops.

Here's another approach: "Nurse, thanks for keeping such a close eye on my blood sugar. Could I just try one of those small Halloween treat-size Snickers? I'll eliminate any other sugar-foods at my next meal. We can both watch to see if my sugar level goes up very much. What do you think?" You've just raised the odds that your nurse will put the chart back on the hook at the end of the bed and check around for a tiny Snickers bar. It is important to realize that, although her outward demeanor is not as friendly as that of some nurses, her underlying interests are most likely to be that you stay as healthy as possible and that the hospital doesn't get sued if you don't. Your need is to satisfy your "sweet tooth." These are not irreconcilable differences. Cross the line with the nurse. Find the common ground rather than "hold your ground."

A word to the nurses out there: We appreciate your skill, your concern, and your excellent care. All we ask is that you continue to be patient with us patients, even when it's about something as simple as a "sweet tooth." We may even settle for few peanut M&Ms, with all that good protein. We'll remember you for the care and for the flexibility as well.

Study the table again with this thought in mind: *You get more when you give a little.* For instance, the *Navigator* needs *time* to think, to analyze, and to decide. If you give him or her a little time to think, the person with a navigator's mindset will not feel rushed. Feeling rushed compromises the quality of his or her thinking and he or she must *think well.* No Navigator worth his or her salt would rush through the plotting of a course of action that will become the methodical key to success. If he did, he could not

201

be sure of the *accuracy* and thoroughness of such a plan. As you allow the Navigator time to think, the chances are he or she will come up with some very sound recommendations for your consideration. Now, reflect on those among your negotiating partners in life who are the "thinkers"—the Navigators? Do you allow them to be good at applying the skills they value most?

This would be a good time to list some of those special negotiating partners in your life—those who will help you get what you need as you help them to succeed.

Partner 1: _____

Partner 2: _____

Partner 3: _____

Partner 4: _____

Using the previous table, reflect on the interactions you have had with these individuals that reveal what is most important to them, so that your combined efforts can be more synergistic. You know from experience that such a commitment on your part will generally increase the probability that others will become committed to helping you get what you need and want.

What About You?

Here's the big question: Do you tend to be the Navigator, Organizer, Facilitator, or Visionary? Does your preoccupation with what you need ever get in the way of helping others succeed? It's called "ego." It is your and my perceived need to control situations to get what we want rather than to create situations in which we attract what we want by winning the trust and the support of others. Remember "crossing the line."

202

Once you've crossed to my side of the line to see my point of view, I am more inclined to walk back to the other side with you to see what's on your side of the world.

Think of yourself, once again, as a magnet. Take a look at the two magnets on the cover of this book. Do you have your positive, attracting energy turned on, or is your negative, repelling energy turned on? When we start from a position of our own needs, the magnet is often turned to "negative" energy, and others feel they are about to be manipulated or controlled. They push back, and now we find ourselves involved in a lose-lose negotiation.

Take some time now to reflect on how you come across to those who are important negotiating partners for you. Is getting what you need important enough that you would be willing to devote an equal amount of energy to helping them get what they need so that you can make them your allies and create that multiplier effect we call teamwork? Most people know the fundamental truth about what will help them succeed. We all learned much of this truth in kindergarten. Sometimes we temporarily forget what we learned and need a periodic reminder. I am thankful for those who lovingly remind me of the truth of what works in getting the most from life, which is so often about giving more to the others you meet along the way—*getting what you need by helping others succeed.*

You, the Communicator

Here's a familiar topic—again. Let's add more to our understanding. If you're going to help others succeed, it is important to know what success means to them. Generally speaking, their measure of success is getting what they want. If you don't know what they want, you cannot help them get it. You've got to ask them and then really listen to the answer. The well-known Tony Robbins says that one of his all-time most powerful questions is to simply ask: "What is especially important to you?" I find that folks are sometimes taken aback when you ask them. Either they're surprised you would be interested or they realize they may not have taken the time to crystallize their own thinking about what is especially important. The question creates a super exercise in rapport building for both the asker and the respondent.

I recently sat in a meeting with a fellow who was very big on his own self-appreciation. At first, he struck me as a wheeler-dealer. At the same time, he was knowledgeable and had a very successful track record in business. I listened and genuinely tried to learn from him as I also tried to figure out if I could come to trust him and like him. Then, he suddenly stopped talking and "blew my mind," if I can use that phrase. He crossed the line and thereby drew me into his corner at the speed of light. He leaned across the table, looked me squarely in the eyes and said, "Darby, what is most important to me in our conversation from this point on is to know what is really important to you. What do you want out of life, and how can I help you get it?" He then sat back in his chair, smiled a genuine smile, and waited patiently for my answer. I could tell he really wanted to hear my answer. I was delighted to have the opportunity to tell him what I really wanted out of life.

Listening is the sincerest form of human recognition. My new friend instantly put me on a pedestal by letting me tell him what was especially important to me. As a result, his potential for influencing me skyrocketed. I did not feel manipulated; I felt appreciated.

Do you care to know what others want? Are you willing to ask? Are you ready to listen? Will it make a difference? **We teach others how to treat us.** As you listen to others tell you what they want, they'll become even more curious about what you want. They will be willing to give you your turn on the pedestal as they respond, in kind, to your genuine interest and to your generosity.

Here is a personal inventory about you, *the communicator...*you, *the listener.* There are certain aptitudes that predispose you to listen and thereby set the stage for more meaningful communication. Please circle H for High, M for Medium, or L for Low to indicate the degree to which your communication effectiveness reflects the following.

Personal Communication Skills Inventory

1.	H – M – L	I believe I know where I stand with others.
2.	H – M – L	I find the beliefs and viewpoints of others to be fascinating.
3.	H – M – L	I can look beyond the personality to appreciate the message.
4.	H – M – L	I am an effective listener.
5.	H – M – L	I can avoid becoming defensive and help others do the same.

6.	H – M – L	I am aware of the impact my words and actions have on others.
7.	H – M – L	It is easy for me to say what is really on my mind.
8.	H – M – L	I am effective at influencing others.
9.	H – M – L	I consciously vary my communication style to adapt to others.
10.	H – M – L	Giving and receiving feedback is a comfortable process.

If you chose *Low* on many of these, you were too hard on yourself. If you chose *High* on most of these, you may be over-confident. If you chose a mix of *High, Medium,* and *Low,* you show yourself to be teachable and willing to work at becoming a better listener and overall communicator. Let's examine some of these 10 items in more depth, starting with item number 4: "I am an effective listener." I once decided that I could not and would not ever mark this item higher than "Medium," because as soon as I perceived myself to be a *great* listener, I might begin telling people what a great listener I am and forget to listen. Effective listening begins with a good dose of humility— to be able to say to yourself: "I know listening is very important. I don't want to take it for granted that I listen well. Only others could evaluate how well they *think* I listen. That is a humbling fact of life."

Let me refer back to my friend in the earlier paragraphs— the one who was initially so self-appreciative, but who turned out to be genuinely interested in what is important to me. In terms of item 6, I don't believe this fellow was aware that I saw him to be a "wheeler-dealer" at first. I think he thought he was simply instructing me. There's a big difference between comingacross as a *helpful instructor* versus coming across as a *wheeler-dealer*. What is the significance of whether he realized this or not? The significance is that he was selling himself short by over-selling himself. How could he have known? He could have checked by simply interjecting this question: "Darby, I wish to share some of the business success principles I've learned, would that be okay?" By doing so, he would have accomplished two very important things: (1) let me know what his agenda was, and (2) by seeking my permission, demonstrate some balance of humility so I wouldn't assume he was just showing off. As he concluded his success stories, he could have asked, "Darby, were those helpful?" At this point, what he would have been doing is about item 1 in the previous inventory, "knowing where you stand with others." And this is all about item 10, "giving and receiving feedback." We now begin to see how these effective communication aptitudes weave together to increase our overall communication effectiveness.

Let's put the shoe on my foot, using the same illustration. The challenge for me relates to item 3 in the inventory: "Can I look beyond the personality to appreciate the message?" My gregarious friend really had much wisdom to share and I needed to get past my initial and mostly unfair "personality assessment" of him to actually *hear* what he was saying that was, in fact, useful and helpful.

At this time, take the opportunity to study and to ponder the 10 items in the inventory to understand what these mean for you. Your effectiveness in these 10 areas will set the stage for being able to relate to others and to engage them in a meaningful way that helps you learn what you need to know to help them succeed. As you establish such rapport, trust will grow, and your influence will be genuinely appreciated.

Pushing Hot Buttons...or Not

If any of us would be an effective influencer, we would be wise to recognize and avoid pushing the "hot buttons" that trigger defensiveness and shut down communication. Let's go back to our conceptual model for understand behavioral preferences, once again.

	Values	Asks	Needs	Buys	Learns From
Navigator	Accuracy	What?	Time	Price/Value	Documentation
Organizer	Predictability	How?	Clarity	Reliability	Checklists
Facilitator	Relationships	Who?	Participation	Enjoyment	Discussion
Visionary	Freedom	Why?	Space	Performance	Experimentation

As you examine each item in each cell of the table, you will discover that there are one or more "hot button" danger points. For instance, take the Navigator. He/she values "Accuracy." A serious hot button would be to diminish the importance of accuracy in any way, especially to put him or her down on the basis of his or her penchant for "being so detail-oriented and thorough." It would also be a hot button to present him or her with shoddy work that represented inattention to details. He or she would go nuts, and perhaps rightly so.

Let's jump around the table a little. Take the Organizer's need for "Clarity." Suppose this person asked you "how" something worked to get the "clarity" she/he needs, and you responded with, "Oh, don't worry, there's several ways that can work. It's not that big a deal. You'll figure it out." Do you know what he or she would be thinking? That you were flaky, and he or she would probably conclude you didn't know *how* whatever it is worked after all. What does he or she need from you? Look to the far right-hand cell on that line of the table. He or she needs a simple checklist of the steps necessary to make the thing work.

This table is a resource for understanding why people get bent out of shape, and how to minimize the probably that they will. Does it mean they're justified in getting bent out of shape? No. What it does mean is that, as an effective communicator and influencer, you want to get off on the right foot with key people in your life and business. Not only do you want to cross the line to relate to them, but you also want to avoid those things that might set them off in a direction that would make them less inclined to value where you're coming from and what you have to offer.

Let's review a couple more examples from the table, just for fun and for learning. Imagine you were selling insurance to a good acquaintance who happened to be somewhat of a Visionary person. What might you inadvertently do that would start things off on the wrong foot? The answer: Fencing him or her in. Remember, she needs space. How might you "fence her in"? You'd fence her in by giving her an insurance form to fill out. You'd be forcing her thinking into a box on a form. Yikes. she likes freedom. Give her space, not a form. Talk about the benefits of the insurance policy. Tell her how easy you'll make it to get the policy she needs processed and in force. Fill the form out for her. Forms are a fenced-in hot button for many people.

On the other hand, your Organizer clients will react in exactly the opposite way to forms. They like forms. In fact, they love to design forms. The Organizer and the Navigator both like documentation. They may ask for your actuarial tables. Give them copies. Study the tables together. Let them fill out their forms and offer to simply check the forms when they're done.

What if, as a parent, you want to give some instruction to your 12-year-old, friendly Facilitator daughter, and she says, "Dad, can we go for a walk while we *discuss* this?" You say, "No, just sit here on the sofa, please." "Ah, come on, Dad, you're no fun," is what she's thinking. She'll sit on the sofa rolling her eyes and tapping her toe on the floor, whereas she would have opened right up as you strolled along the sidewalk, as she *enjoyed* the fresh air outdoors. Cross the line with your kids and discover the magic.

You're probably asking yourself, "Do I need to be some sort of amateur psychologist to avoid people's hot buttons and to relate to them so that I can have some positive influence with them?" The answer is no, you don't. All you need to do is to be more observant in a most friendly and caring way. Observe how people approach you and what they are truly saying when they communicate. Two examples follow. Pay close attention to the words people use that convey what their real needs are in terms of how they hope you will respond.

Example One: Suppose someone at work approaches you cautiously and says, "I don't understand this task. Can you please take a minute to discuss this with me?" [Key words: "take a minute" and "discuss."] Here's a *disconnect*: "I'm sort of busy. I can just send you an e-mail later with some instructions on how it's to be done, if that's okay." Instead, you will score big points if you just take a minute to discuss it with him or her. Yes, this means you *take a minute to discuss it*—not send an e-mail with a checklist. He or she needs to be involved and to participate with you in a discussion. You can make it a brief discussion, but friendly nevertheless. This investment in him or her will yield positive dividends for you both in the days ahead.

Example Two: The opposite situation. Someone else asks for your help...."I'm not sure I understand this task. Would you please create a checklist of what I'm supposed to do?" [Key word: "checklist."] Disconnect: "It's much easier to just tell you. Sit down. I'll explain; it's really quite simple." This person actually wants a checklist. That's what he or she said. So, you say, "Great, I've got a checklist. Let me e-mail it to you as soon as I get back to my desk." He or she wants it in writing for a variety of reasons, and you can save yourself some time by just sending the email. What if you don't have a checklist? Make one. Now you've got two ways of explaining whatever this task is, which means to you can relate to at least two types of people and how they best respond to instructions. You are now twice as powerful at influencing others when you have options that are suited to their needs and interests.

211

People actually do signal from where they're coming and how they need to interact with you by how they approach you and what they say. You don't need a Ph.D. in psychology; all you need is to have your radar—your powers of observation—turned on to pick up the signals. What is the biggest obstacle? How busy we all are. Most of us are so busy rushing here and there that we think we don't have time to turn on the radar. What happens instead is misunderstandings and miscommunication that end up creating bigger problems that take even more of our time to fix and get right. Wouldn't it be great if we would just slow down for each other, take a deep breath, and simply say, "Let me be sure I understand what you're telling me and how I can help."

Passive–Aggressive–Assertive

It doesn't seem that training in this area is as prevalent as it was a number of years ago, but it is helpful to understand three postures we accidentally take or can deliberately employ in approaching others. To begin this discussion, consider the legend of Superman. Remember Clark Kent? He was *passive*. Remember Lex Luthor? He was *aggressive*. Remember Superman? He was *assertive*. (And what about Lois Lane? I'll leave that determination up to you.) This discussion sort of connects us back to the discussion of parent, adult, and child. Parent dominates. Child is intimidated. Adult takes action. When presuming to exert a positive influence with others to get what you need by helping them succeed, it is very useful to be aware of posturing—yours and that of your communication partners as well. Here is a table to help....

212

	Passive Posture	Aggressive Posture	Assertive Posture
Beliefs and General Characteristics	o "I must be nice." • Apologetic. o Quick to acquiesce. • Needs to survive.	o "I've got rights." • Always achieves goals. o The end justifies the means. • Needs to control.	o "We're in this together." • Moves forward. o Learns from each step. • Needs to make some progress.
Verbal: The words you choose and the phrases you use.	o "Yes, whatever you think is important." • "I hope...." o "Don't worry." • "Sorry."	o "You have to...." • "This is the way it's done." o "You just don't understand."	o "This appears to be the issue." • "What do you think?" o "How can we make this work?"
Nonverbal: Body Posture, Face/Eyes, Gestures, Tone of Voice, Pace.	o Wrings hands. • Hand over mouth o Eyes wander. • Speaks slowly, softly.	o Points a finger. • Abrupt movements. o Intense eye contact. • Speaks very quickly.	o Energized. • Reaches out. o Comfortable eye contact. • Conversational.

Do you see any behaviors that are familiar in the previous table? With this table in mind, consider that two of the most important words in understanding what it takes to become a more effective communicator are *Equal* and *Unequal.* When relationships and interactions are on *equal* footing, things will generally work out. When relationships and interactions are on *unequal* footing, somebody or something's going to slip. It is easy to see from the table that taking an aggressive posture will often create an "unequal" situation and result in the intimidation of those who are in a more passive or even assertive posture. The passive person's response will be to acquiesce. The assertive person's response may be a little "put off," but she will attempt to create a constructive discussion of the issues.

The opportunity for the passive individual is to move gradually toward a more assertive set of behaviors. You probably realize that the greatest potential for productivity and creative problem solving is when two or more individuals are relatively assertive in speaking up and addressing the issues at hand. But you're also probably wondering how an equal relationship between two passive individuals or two aggressive individuals will ultimately work out. Two passive individuals will retire to the sofa, turn on the TV, and enjoy sharing a bowl of popcorn. Two aggressive individuals will duke it out and eventually choose to avoid each other, or possibly see the futility of their warlike posturing. At least the power struggle will be on equal footing. And, it is possible that they actually enjoy the rush of adrenalin that combat produces.

What is the message here? It is simply to be aware of postures and posturing and to either accept the natural outcome of what you inadvertently choose, or be *more assertive* in choosing to be more assertive. When "assertive" is done well, you don't have much to lose. By contrast, a passive posture won't get you very far, and it is too easy to succumb to a victim mentality as a result. If you habitually slip into an aggressive posture, you may win a few battles, but find yourself to be a lonely man or woman. They may say this about you; "It isn't that he never had any friends, he's just used them all."

The passive individual gives in to others and will do whatever it takes to avoid rejection. This also means that the passive individual will seldom take risks. The aggressive individual needs to control others to be sure there is no deviation from his or her intended goal. Nearly any risk is acceptable as long as the goal is achieved. Even relationships will be sacrificed in the interest of following the agenda and reaching the goal. The assertive individual is more concerned with progress and positive outcomes. Outcomes are measured on a relative basis that allows for trade-offs that may differ from the original goal. The assertive individual realizes that the way to get more done is to work with and through others. Thus, it is about _getting what you need by helping others succeed._ Outcomes are results. Relationships represent key resources for creating these outcomes.

Discipline Is Remembering What You Want

One of my all-time favorite insights is this: _Discipline is remembering what you want._ If we fail to get what we need out of life, it is because we forgot what we wanted in the first place. Significant "wants" are the result of our deepest desires. Once we harness this passion, we will become creative in finding the ways to achieve our goals and create the overall results that we truly need. You will now ask about the aggressive person who is goal-driven. The energy of an aggressive person is a powerful thing. As I said, an aggressive person can win the battle, even if she wins it all on her own. But here comes an especially powerful insight: To maximize success in life, it is important to know both _what you want_ and _what you really want._

215

Let's consider the work-related example of a sales manager. For a few minutes, put yourself in the shoes of a sales manager. You may say that what you want is to meet a sales quota. It is highly probable that what you *really* want is to enjoy the lifestyle that meeting your sales quota will allow you to enjoy. You also want to build a superior sales team to help you exceed the sales quota month in and month out. You realize that merely meeting a sales quota isn't enough, and that building a sales team will allow you to multiply your own efforts with even more rewarding results. This prompts special discipline as a sales team leader. You realize that to push aggressively for the sales goal and to alienate your sales team in the process would be self-defeating in the long term. Thus, you choose an assertive and inspirational approach to leading your team rather than a hard-driving and aggressive approach. *What you really want* is a highly motivated and skillful sales team that will make it easier for you to achieve your dream. This is a far more powerful motive than to just meet and exceed some sales quota. Rather than be driven to mere short-term results, you will be lifted to a more strategic approach to more lasting sales success.

When you or I put on the aggressive posture, the ego is in charge. When we put on an assertive posture, we become a disciplined problem solver with a more strategic view of things. We also place greater value on the relationships we have with others as we realize that they are often the key to our own successes. Your sales team is more important than the sales quota. They are the key to the success you seek.

Defining Your Problem-Solving Mission

As you embark on getting what you want and need and as you set out to do the problem solving that is required, consider these dimensions of defining your mission: Start with what is popularly called a "gap analysis." Identify what *is* happening in your current situation that is different from what you believe *could be* happening. This will result in a problem statement, even an opportunity statement, about closing the gap.

Once you've done your "gap analysis," write some problem-solving/decision-making goals along these lines: Ask yourself what you hope to *Achieve,* to *Preserve,* and to *Avoid as potential problems* by whatever you choose to do in closing the gaps you see and facing the challenges that lie before you. Such objectives will help prevent the short-sightedness that can result in winning the battle and losing the war or in achieving your sales quota and alienating your sales team in the process. Address these questions:

o What do I/we need to *achieve* by whatever course of action we choose? (List these.) These are interim outcomes or progress milestones.

• What do we need to *preserve* by whatever course of action we choose? (List these.) These are favorable conditions, values, and relationships that are not worth sacrificing.

o What do we need to *avoid* as problems by whatever we do? (List these.) These are the pitfalls you need to avoid through greater vigilance and sensitivity.

Let's suppose you and your team are setting out to break your previous sales record for total business booked in a single month. What would be your *opportunity statement*, based on your *gap analysis*? Is there a gap or purely a "moving to the next level" opportunity? To help guide you on your way, how would your interim *Achieve, Preserve,* and *Avoid* problem-solving, decision-making, and results-achieving objectives look and sound? Here are some examples:

Achieve

- o A clearly relevant solution for each customer to build confidence quickly and to assure overall customer satisfaction.
- An efficient order-entry process to assure overall timeliness and a swift delivery of our products.
- o Solid customer confidence that we are market leaders, to encourage repeat business and multiple orders in a short time frame.

Preserve

- o My/our reputation for ethical conduct and overall professionalism.
- Goodwill and efficient communication with all of our marketing partners—internal and external.

218

o Customer confidence in our ability to recognize their needs and to represent these to the rest of the company.

Avoid

o Appearing to be overly aggressive.

• Failing to touch base with various company departments that must support the sale.

o Trashing our competitors.

Can you see the value of such an exercise? If you commit to such a blueprint of action before you start, you will have an underlying sensitivity to many important issues that will avoid unnecessary conflict and assure a set of outcomes that are positive, both in the short term and in the long term. As you work with your team and your customers, you will be the world-class problem solver, friendly influencer, sales orchestrator, company ambassador, go-to person, and team player you intend to be. The special interim objectives (APA: Achieve, Preserve, Avoid) are about "safely treading where angels otherwise fear to tread." What does this familiar statement actually mean? It means that angels are smart enough to know there are some places you don't go, or that, if you go there, you have your eyes wide open. There are risks and there are *calculated risks*. Taking a calculated risk means you have done your homework and have your eyes wide open. This is what makes you brave enough to stretch farther and to reach higher than those who are more passive and would not dare to try.

Force Field Analysis

As you adjust your personal posture for maximum positive influence, you increase the overall positive energy for getting done what you need to get done that also benefits others. You increase your ability to transform opposition into innovation.

Let's look further at how you can maximize the *Driving Forces* that are working in your favor and minimize or eliminate the *Restraining Forces* that would block your progress. Think of these forces, respectively, as the accelerator on an automobile and as the brakes on an automobile. If you want to move forward, you've got to press on the accelerator and also make sure the brakes are released. Here is a simple tool to amplify your success as you prepare to negotiate with others—as you work to influence and to support others in achieving what's important to them.

		Idea/Want/Need		
Driving Forces	➔ ➔ ➔	Desired Outcome	⬅ ⬅ ⬅	*Restraining Forces*

Identify and list the Driving Forces that will help you "make it happen." Accentuate these. Identify and list the Restraining Forces. Go to work to minimize or eliminate these. Other people, with their opinions, behavioral preferences, and problem-solving postures, will represent most of the Driving Forces and most of the Restraining Forces as well. This is why the whole process has so much to do with you as the communicator. It's all about people. The only way to solve problems and make progress with people is through effective communication.

Here's an example of a Force Field Analysis. Let's return to our sales manager illustration. So, you want to meet and exceed your sales quota and you want to beat your "previous best" sales record. Congratulations. Here is an initial list of Driving and Restraining Forces that will affect your goal:

Driving Forces	Restraining Forces
1. The recent, high-powered sales training seminar you just attended.	1. It is summer with lots of vacations scheduled (your team, customer contacts).
2. The new feature of your #1 product that was just announced to enhance serviceability.	2. Your chief competitor has just lowered its price by 8 percent.
3. Approval of the new sales bonus program.	3. The accounting department just tightened the restrictions on entertaining customers.

The Balance of Power

Most of us hope to have some level of power and influence in this world. As we have discussed, *power* is the ability to get things done—to make things happen. *Influence* is the ability to enlist others in the cause. There is often a tug of war between people—a "power play" as they attempt to enlist each other's participation and support. You will experience greater success at influencing as you recognize the *balance of power* and turn it to a strategic advantage. The power individuals

221

wield comes in many forms: position power, institutional author-ity, force of personality, sheer intelligence, the weight of the re-sources at their disposal, prestige and stature, goodness, earned respect, the power of persuasion, and more. It is a fascinating list. It is important to have a healthy respect for each of these "points of personal power." There is also the important opportunity to cultivate these for your own success in life. You can readily iden-tify and contrast those forms of personal power that are aggres-sive and intimidate others versus those that are assertive and are more likely to engage others and to persuade them.

The exercise of power is situational. For instance, if you are a highway patrol officer and someone is speeding, you can rightfully use your *institutional authority* to change the situation as you write out a citation and specify a "painful" penalty. At the same time, I am relieved when I encounter an officer who sizes up the situation, realizes that I am not a major threat to society, and just gives me a friendly yet firm warning, rather than a speeding ticket.

If you're playing a game of chess, *the weight of the resources* at your disposal is always a key power factor. The more knights, rooks, bishops, and pawns you hang on to, the better. Con-versely, those weighty resources can be quickly overcome by the *sheer intelligence* of your opponent. One smart move puts you in a position of stalemate and your options are suddenly and seriously limited.

Given the many and varied situations we all face in life, it is likely that most of us will use most of these forms of personal power at some time or another. Choose wisely. Choose to exercise power with these two broad criteria in mind:

1. What will help me to be more effective in the situation at hand?

2. What will also have the most positive long-term benefits. In other words, don't be short-sighted?

For example, a parent can often win out over a child by the power of parental authority and the force of an adult personality. However, potential loss of trust in that child may be far too great a price to pay. Thus, you and I will choose to moderate our approaches with our children and to begin our interactions with them on the basis of kindness and gentle persuasion. *When you exert control over your children (and others), the effect is temporary. It lasts until you leave the room. When you influence your children (and others), the effect can last a lifetime.*

To maximize the practical value of this book, let's take this concept of "Balance of Power" to a situational level. Let's presume that you are entering a serious negotiation at work, in business, or otherwise. Here is a tool to help you analyze the situations you encounter and to adjust the balance of power as needed. It will strengthen your influence and also allow you to keep the playing field sufficiently level that others believe they can achieve what is important to them as well. Note: I grant that there may be extreme situations you encounter that are a matter of survival—literally or figuratively. In these situations you may want the field to be uneven because the cost of losing the negotiation is simply unacceptable. Hopefully, most of us don't face such severe consequences all that often. Thus, the long-term need to sustain positive relationships with our negotiating partners can temper our "winner take all" mentality. Here's the tool:

The Balance of Power

Key Factors	You—0—Negotiating Partner(s)	Strategy for Better Balance
Strength of the Need	5 - 4 - 3 - 2 - 1 - **0** - 1 - 2 - 3 - 4 - 5	(Make your plans.)
Strength of the Argument	5 - 4 - 3 - 2 - 1 - **0** - 1 - 2 - 3 - 4 - 5	(Make your plans.)
Points of Personal Power	5 - 4 - 3 - 2 - 1 - **0** - 1 - 2 - 3 - 4 - 5	(Make your plans.)
The Weight of Knowledge	5 - 4 - 3 - 2 - 1 - **0** - 1 - 2 - 3 - 4 - 5	(Make your plans.)
Pressure: Time/ Resources	5 - 4 - 3 - 2 - 1 - **0** - 1 - 2 - 3 - 4 - 5	(Make your plans.)
Overall Force Field	5 - 4 - 3 - 2 - 1 - **0** - 1 - 2 - 3 - 4 - 5	(Make your plans.)

Instructions: Consider each of the Key Factors and indicate your assessment as to whether the balance of power is in the direction of "You" or your "Negotiating Partner(s)." Circle the representative number on the 5-point, bi-directional scale. Perhaps you will perceive a neutral balance and indicate a "0" or midpoint assessment.

Footnotes—Key Factors:

1. *Strength of the Need* is about the importance of each party's overall proposition. For instance, if you are debating whether to create an irrigation

224

canal that will run behind your house, which is intended to supply the needs of a thousand farmers, the balance of power is not in your favor.

2. *Strength of the Argument* is about the credibility of your proposition versus the propositions others make. If you have the testimony of three angry neighbors and the proponent of the canal has a 600-page U.S. Department of Agriculture study of the economic and environmental impacts, the balance of power still favors construction of the canal.

3. *Points of Personal Power* is about all the possible forms and expressions of your individual power that we discussed in the preceding paragraphs. Study these. How can you strengthen your personal credibility and persuasiveness?

4. *The Weight of Knowledge* is the weight of the facts, which means that she or he with the most data and information has a favorable balance of power in the negotiating arena.

5. *Pressure: Time and Resources* is about the urgency of things and the availability of resources. Back to the canal analogy. If the community has been studying the canal for three years and the decision must be made today, your probability of winning the argument is lessened. Time is running out—the time to get more data, to deliberate, to find more neighbors to testify on your behalf, and

so on. *Resources* is about who has the money and the wherewithal to pull it off—in other words, who has the bucks and the bulldozers.

6. *Overall Force Field* is a summary of all the factors you can think of that will strengthen the probability that your proposal will get a fair hearing and that you will have some influence on the outcome of things.

You may look at the example of the canal behind your home and ask, "What power can I possibly have in an argument with the captains of the local economy and the federal government?" This is the very point of this "Balance of Power" exercise, to not give up, but to better prepare yourself to improve your odds of success—of being a force for good where there are multiple sides to an argument that need to be constructively aired and heard. You may not stop the canal from being built, but, by the strength of your conviction and the quality of your presentation, you can increase the commitment to protect and beautify the environment that surrounds the canal. You can help assure that its inevitable impact takes into account the diverse interests of those who will be affected by its presence. You will accomplish this by looking out for your own backyard and those of your neighbors, *and* by being fully enlightened and objective about the importance of the canal to the family farms and agricultural businesses in your area.

Adversaries and Enemies

An important sidenote at this point in the book would be this: *Do not be too quick to define others as your adversaries or enemies.* Earlier, we discussed the propensity we humans have for taking hard and fast positions—for drawing lines in the sand and forbidding others to cross these lines or be smitten. With our hard and fast positions, we polarize each other. Anger is the result. When we are angry, we are not effective negotiators. At such times, we become egotistical brutes who do no real good. We only create for ourselves that isolation rightfully reserved for egotistical people.

In the Dalai Lama's book *The Art of Happiness*, he teaches that anger and calm cannot exist simultaneously in the mind. Even in the face of his would-be enemies, the Dalai Lama is calm. He offers this insight: "The enemy is a very good teacher." In fact, the one who is calm can observe the would-be enemy to understand how best to win over that enemy by not defeating him at all." What strategies for winning come out of anger? None. What strategies for winning come out of calmness? All strategies for winning come from intelligent reflection. Here is a strategy for winning the influence you seek. Once again, it is to shun "the tyranny of the *or*"—that our answers must be either yes or no. Lines in the sand are physical manifestations of "the tyranny of the *or*." Either you cross the line or you don't. If you cross the line, you may die. If you do not cross the line, you are psychologically defeated. This is not a strategy for winning influence. This is a strategy for losing everything in the end.

227

It is only by "crossing the line" that there is any genuine understanding of what's on the other side. So, to exaggerate the polarizing ultimatums of *black or white, right or wrong, do or die* is to accept our own ignorance of where others stand and why. To win, you must invite your would-be adversaries to visit your side of the line. If they are reluctant to do so, tell them you would like to visit their side of the line to learn more. As you observe things on "the other side," you will expand your capability for devising creative options to turn opposition into innovation. Success need never be an exclusive prize. As you share success, your own success will be multiplied. As you are governed by the laws of abundance rather than by the laws of scarcity, you will be liberated by your own generosity.

A Prayer Room for My Friends

I recall my trips to Southeast Asia and to Africa, to countries and regions where people of Islamic, Buddhist, or Hindu faith are a majority. I remember one seminar in Kuala Lumpur. I was teaching under the auspices of a British company whose representatives had meticulously arranged our breaks with tea, biscuits, mineral water, and soda. These breaks were held in a lovely, elegantly draped room near the conference room where we met. Midway through the first break, one of my most conscientious students approached me and asked, "Mr. Checketts, at the next break, can we please have a prayer room for Muslims to take their break?" I felt an instantaneous and fortunately short-lived twinge in my neck as if I had somehow been challenged for failing to adequately accommodate our seminar participants. I admit that the thought which flashed through my mind in a microsecond was, "We do tea breaks—not prayer breaks—because that's what the British do." Wisely, the words that came out of my mouth meant I had caught myself in time to cross the cultural line I needed to cross. To the request for a "prayer room," I replied, "Certainly, we can arrange that." As I went to the hotel manager's office, I suddenly felt myself embarking on an ambassadorial mission to accommodate my international guests. After all, my assignment was to influence each and every person who had come to our seminar from many different professions, industries, nations, and cultures.

As I walked back to the seminar room, I thought to myself that perhaps I could also do with a prayer on the next break. What's more, I had probably eaten too many biscuits and had too much soda at our previous western-style break. When time came for our afternoon intermission, I went for a quiet walk in the courtyard and whispered my own prayer there. I didn't kneel down. I just looked upward and said, "God, thanks for this amazing multicultural adventure. Help me to teach well."

Revisit: Agree in Principle

As you seek creative ways to win influence and move your deliberations and negotiations with others forward, remember the power of "agreeing in principle." Based on the underlying interests people hold versus their stated positions, you can open new windows of opportunity where there might otherwise be stubborn opposition. To illustrate, if your vice president of operations states that you must reduce inventories at your regional distribution center, you can debate the issue as two positions on inventory: the same level *or* a lower level. There are your two positions. The alternative approach is to ask your vice president what's driving the inventory discussion. We all know there's an 80 percent chance it is a need to reduce operating costs. Ask your VP how much money needs to come out of your budget. Let's say it's 6 percent. Your next statement moves away from the inventory discussion to say, "Boss, if I can find a way to save 6 percent or more without reducing inventory levels, will you consider my proposal?" This simple question initiates the powerful process of obtaining *agreement in principle* without getting stuck in a debate over the two opposing positions that you and your boss otherwise hold regarding inventory.

This approach opens up the options. Is this common sense? Yes. Do many of you reading this book instinctively take this approach from time to time? Yes. Do most of us remember to take this approach often enough? No. As smart as we all are, we still fall into the trap of defending our positions rather than recognizing that there are many alternative ways to satisfy the underlying interests of others—ways that do not result in a win-lose situation for any of the parties involved. In the previous scenario, your boss achieves lower operating costs and you still have the inventory needed to meet the quick turnaround demands of your customers. Remember "tree hugging"? This approach is the antidote for tree hugging.

In summary, please refer back to this chapter for those conceptual "tools" that will support your commitments to others as you also build the influence you need to have. Together with Chapter 8, this chapter provides a basis for planning and preparing for those important communication opportunities we all face. Your reputation as an effective communicator will grow, and you will be seen as one who can assist others as they transform opposition into innovation. It has been said, "You can have great ideas, but without influence and without the support of others, these may never see the light of day." Your ideas and mine are so much of who we are. As we move past our conflicts to find the energy inside, the light will be there.

Conclusion
When Sparks Fly, They Light Up the Sky

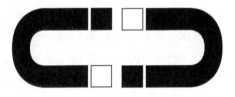

Imagine a world without conflict. There'd be no getting over being angry. There'd be no opportunities to "kiss and make up." The news would be boring. And, one of my family counselor friends said, "If there were no open conflict, I couldn't help a family in trouble." She went on to explain that *open* conflict in a family means ideas are being aired and tested. At least people know what others are thinking, even if it is in the form of disagreement. She says, "Once the conflict happens, we begin to discover where we need to go next." Perhaps a family that experiences no conflict is "holding it in" and letting it fester...or, is it possible that they are unnaturally tranquil and therefore not likely to be very creative at problem solving?

I think we humans are simply too colorful, creative, and full of energy to placidly agree with each other all the time.

The problem isn't the conflict itself, it is that we too often and too easily "freak out" when it happens. That's why there's a book entitled *Positive Conflict*. Next time your family is having some conflict, look at each other and say, "I read a book that says there's energy inside all this and that our conflict is a sign we are a creative family. Let's turn our opposition into innovation."

It is not uncommon that the conflicts we have with each other begin in the same manner as those fireworks on New Year's Eve. They go off with a sometimes scary boom and then light up the sky. When conflict occurs we have two opportunities: (1) We can demonstrate our clear presence of mind and our skill at handling the "stuff" that happens in life and/or (2) we can rediscover that conflict is the way individuals test the diversity of their ideas—to be who they are and to hope others will cut them some slack. Our disagreement opens the dialogue that ultimately produces a new level of understanding and reveals creative new angles on the problems we face together.

Handling the Stuff
That Happens With Skill

A friend of mine told me he had learned a simple phrase that saved his marriage. It is: "That's interesting." My friend admitted that he had been prone to create conflict with his spouse by how he reacted to the problems that occurred. He would overreact and the sparks would fly. He decided that the next time there was a problem in the course of their daily coming and going he would simply observe the situation and say to himself: "That's interesting, I wonder what I can learn from this." The very next crisis to hit his family was for his wife to have a fender-bender on the way home from work. She telephoned her husband and fearfully explained what had happened, expecting him to blow up. Instead, he simply said, "I'll be right there." He drove to where the damaged car was parked and saw her standing there timidly anticipating his arrival. He calmly got out of the car and walked toward her. As he looked at the dents in the car, he remarked, "That's interesting," and stroked his chin. She waited for him to say more. He did not. He smiled at her. She ran forward and put her arms around his neck as she sobbed and said, "I love you." He told me that was a turning point in their marriage.

Testing the Diversity of Our Ideas

Our ideas are what make us distinctly human. These ideas are about our individual sense of identity and purpose. These ideas are about others, our relationships to them, and our shared commitments. These ideas are about what's possible, and our potential for success and happiness. It is the formulating of ideas and thinking about these ideas that sets us apart from the zebras, chimpanzees, and dolphins. Rather than act on instinct alone, we choose our paths through life. We probe to discover. We test our ideas. We make plans and we act. Yes, sometimes we act impulsively as if without thinking, and yet our impulses are still a reflection of the thinking and the experiencing we have previously done that have shaped our natural inclinations to act.

Because we create our worlds by how we each think about the world, we want our ideas to be sound. Thus, we find ways to test our ideas. What are these ways? We ask. We make propositions to influence others. We watch for the reactions of others. We experiment. We research and compare our ideas with those who have gone before us or who possess special wisdom. When we test our ideas, we presume to be open to the possibility that some ideas are not as likely to work as others. When we are not open, we become defensive and create conflict. As we face the reality that the ideas of others often differ from our own, we encounter disagreement, and there may be conflict. And yet, all of this is a *testing process*. How do we pass the test? We can choose to make what is called a paradigm shift.

A paradigm is a conceptual model or a mental picture we hold of how we think things are supposed to be out there in the world. Making a paradigm shift is to simply discover that you own the "channel changer" for your life. You can shift to another paradigm as quickly as you can change the channels on your remote control to view a different picture on the television screen. To illustrate, you can test an idea on a teammate at work and get "push back." The paradigm we often hold is that others should more quickly see the merit in our ideas. Therefore, *push back* is saying, "I don't like your idea." A paradigm shift produces this: *Push back* may also be saying,

"I'm just not ready for your idea." So, rather than engage in conflict with your teammate, you realize that you have more homework and friendly persuading to do to help him or her get ready to support your idea.

The subtitle of this book suggests a major paradigm shift. Refer again to the illustration of the two magnets on the cover. The magnets can be positioned so that the polar opposites do not repel. Correctly applied, the power of the two magnets can attract and ultimately draw two force fields together. A personal paradigm shift is to realize that opposition is a test as to whether we can shape our own ideas to fit and to meld with the creative input of others. By so doing, we can attract the support we really want.

After the sparks fly, we do light up the sky. This is the moment when we cry "Eureka!" and declare a breakthrough in our abilities to solve problems and build better relationships.

Recommended Reading

The following books are some of my favorites. The special significance of their listing here is that they have directly influenced the formulation of the principles and practices of **Positive Conflict**. Some are newer books; some are older and so full of wisdom...and well worth tracking down wherever they may be found.

A classic that conveys the practical principles of influencing and negotiating in a modern age....

Getting to Yes by Roger Fisher and William Ury (Random House Business Books, 2003)

One of the latest in the library of spirit-lifting books created by my marvelous coach....

The Story of You...And How to Create a New One by Steve Chandler (Career Press, 2006)

A book to free your mind...to let *calm* enter where *anger* may have been....

The Art of Happiness by His Holiness the Dalai Lama and Howard C. Cutler (Riverhead Books, 1998)

The book that most helped me understand my dispositions and those of my fellow travelers....

The Creative Brain by the late Ned Herrmann, who was the mentor's mentor (Ned Herrmann Group, 1989)

A true-life book that opened my eyes about cultural differences and cultural conflict....

From Beirut to Jerusalem by Thomas Friedman (HarperCollins Publishers, 1998)

A landmark and *perspective-changing* book on leadership....

Stewardship by Peter Block (Berrett-Koehler Publishers, 1993)

One of the most "broaden your thinking" business books ever written....

Built to Last by James Collins and Jerry Porras (HarperBusiness, 1997)

Perhaps one of the most important modern books you might possibly ever read....

The End of Poverty by Jeffrey D. Sachs (Penguin, 2006)

Index

A

absolutes, 180-190, 193
abundance mentality, 50-51
abundance, laws of, 228
achievement vs. contentment, 108
achieving mastery, 102
acknowledging others, 62
ACT, 132
adult mode, 120
agreeable, being, 131-134, 180
agreeing in principle, 229-231
agreement in principle, 127-128
agreements, tracking your, 129-131
Al-haji, 166
ambiguity, 119
analysis paralysis, 146
animosity towards others, 52
APA (Achieve, Preserve, Avoid), 219

Apollo 13 lunar mission, 92, 96
Apple, 168-169
Arnold, John, 180
arrogance and paranoia, 60
Art of Communication, Masters of, 115-117
Art of Happiness, The, 227
art of
    life, the, 114-115
    negotiation, the, 45
    reconciliation, the, 114
attraction of opposites, the, 137-138
avoiding conflict, 72

B

Balance of Power concept, 223, 226
basics of communication effectiveness, 116
"been there, done that" syndrome, 30
being agreeable, 131-134, 180

belief, 93
bonding energy, 24
Buddha, 166, 176
Built to Last, 97

C

cascade of wisdom, 61
child mode, 120-121
civilization, definition of, 158
closed-ended questions vs. open-
    ended questions, 76-77
Collins, Jim, 97, 108
collisions of life, the, 41
commitment to listen, the, 80
common interests, 190
communication, 113-136
comprehensive solutions, 35
compromises, opportunity for, 50
conflict avoidance, 71-72
conflict,
    avoiding, 72
    interpersonal, 128
conflict-to-conquest scenario, 51
contentment vs. achievement, 108
control vs. influence, 55-56
coping behaviors, 140
corner on the truth, having a, 184-194
corporate culture, 168-169
Covey, Dr. Stephen, 29, 50
Creative Brain, The, 143
critical thinking vs. provisional
    thinking, 98
crossing the line, 201, 203-204, 210
    importance of, 146

cultural opposites, 157
culture clashes, 171
culture, definition of, 158
customer problem solving, 78

D

dealing with
    difficult people, 72-75
    interests, not positions, 180
diagonal opposites, 146
dichotomies, 95, 107
    ideological, 180
    overreacting to, 96
    dichotomous
    pairs, 111
    situation, a, 107
dichotomy, a perfect, 106
difficult people, dealing with, 72-75
dilemmas, 88-89
diplomatic approach to minimizing
    conflict, the, 123
Driving Forces, 220
dynamic tension, 87

E

effective communication aptitudes, 207
"Effective Interviewing" course, 75
element of trust, 118
employee-supervisor relationships, 78
End of Poverty, The, 171
energy,
    human atomic, 31
    nuclear, 24
energy inside conflict, the, 116, 134

energy inside,
  finding the, 231, 36, 150-151
extreme, taking thing to the, 109
extremism in government, 42
extroverts, 140

F

Facilitator, the, 141, 144-149, 152, 199-200, 202, 210
fear, 90-91
  facing, 91
fickle, being, 82-86
fight fire with fire, 73
Five Arenas of Life, the, 177-179
5 Ws, the, 75-80
Force Field Analysis, 221
four,
  dimensions of behavioral preferences, 143
  quadrants of brain functionality, 142
four-quadrant conceptual model, the, 143, 147
fusing atoms, 25
fusion, an opportunity for, 26
fusion of ideas, the, 113

G

gap analysis, 217-218
generalities vs. specifics, 74
genius of the *and*, the, 97-98, 178
getting to yes/yes, 134
guilt trip, definition of, 184
guilt trips, 184-186
Gutenberg, Johann, 154-156

H

helpful instructor vs. wheeler-dealer, 207
Herrmann, Ned, 141-142, 144
hope, 93
hoping, 90
hot buttons, 208-212
human atomic energy, 31
human spirit, leveraging, 176
humility, 62
  definition of, 111

I

idealism, 192
ideas, the power of, 27
ideological
  dichotomies, 180
  opposites, 183-184
Industrial Age, the, 176
influence vs. control, 55-56
influence, definition of, 221
Information Age, the, 176
inner conflicts, 88
interests vs. positions, 125-127
internal conflict, 86-88
interpersonal conflict, 128
inter-view, 79
introverts, 141

L

laid-back extrovert, the, 141
laws of
  abundance, 228
  scarcity, 228
leader, the perfect, 102
leadership dichotomies, 109-111

left-brain, idea of the, 142

lines in the sand, drawing, 123

listening, 119

emphasis on, 114

Lun, Ts'ai, 154-156, 164

M

magic words,
four, 70-71, 77
three, 76-77

Master of Dichotomies, becoming a, 95, 101-111

Masters of the Art of Communication, 115-117

maximum allocation of resources, 181

minimum standard of performance, 181

multiple
perspectives, 42-46
points of view, 35

mutual exclusiveness of ideas, a, 30

N

nationalism, 167-168

Navigator, the, 141, 144-148, 152, 199-202, 208, 210

naysayers, 30

negotiating
skill, 198
skills, 46

negotiating, 198

9/11, 166, 174

"not listening," avoiding, 64

nuclear,
energy, 24
fission, 24
fusion, 25, 105

O

off-balance approach, an, 106

Oliver, story of, 81-87, 91, 114

open conflict, 233

open-ended questions vs. closed-ended questions, 76-77

opportunity statement, 218

opposition into innovation,
transforming, 127, 147, 157, 159, 172, 175, 180-181, 192-193, 197, 220, 234
turning, 107, 116, 134, 151

optimist, the, 91-94, 96, 132, 151

optimists, 85

Organizer, the, 141, 144, 146, 148-149, 152, 199-200, 202, 209-210

origin of ideas, respect for, 62

P

P&C&ALH, 125

paper, the invention of, 154, 156, 164

paradigm shift, 32, 236-237

paradigm, definition of, 236

parent mode, 120-121

parent, adult, and child, 212

parent-child tone, 122

perceiving a way through, 104

perceptiveness, 103

Personal Communication Skills Inventory, 205

personality clash, 137

personality dispositions, 140

pessimist, the, 91, 93, 95, 132, 151

pessimists, 85

Peters, Tom, 30

Pilot, the, 144-145, 148

platitudes, definition of, 192

points of personal power, 222

politics, 189-193

positions vs. interests, 125-127

potential value in opposing ideas, the, 35

power of

belief, the, 94

ideas, the, 27

Power of

Opposites, the, 36, 95, 107, 111, 113, 141, 143, 146

Personality Opposites, 148

power, definition of, 111, 221

pre-call the situation, 54

prejudice, 113

preventive action, 71

principles of optimism, 114

Principles of Team Conduct, 194

developing your, 151

printing press, invention of the, 155

prior agreements, 129

process efficiencies, 96

procrastination, 90

Pros & Cons & Argue Like Heck, 125

provisional thinking vs. critical thinking, 98

provisional thinking, 32

prudence, 107

purchasing process, the, 148

push back, 236

R

rapport, 118, 129

reader of people, being a, 117

realist, the, 91-95

redirect your energies, 120

reinvent the wheel, having to, 34

religion, 186-189

religions of the world, 165-167

reserve judgment, 89, 163, 179

resistance training, 38

Restraining Forces, 220

right-brain, idea of the, 142

risk-taking selves, our, 86

Robbins, Tony, 204

S

Sachs, Jeffrey, 171

safeguarding selves, our, 86

scarcity mentality, 29, 50, 55

scarcity, laws of, 228

self-deterministic consultants, 108

seven methods and commitments, 116

shared ideas, 59

Sharia, 170-171

silence, 118-119

smelling the roses, 109

special interests, 190

specifics vs. generalities, 74

spirit of

teamwork, definition of the, 196

unity, the, 176

spiritual commitment, 177

standards of ethics, decency, or personal safety, 73

stereotyping others, 139

strawberry, the power inside a, 24-26

stubbornness, 104

superficial agreement, 34

T

"taking advantage" of others, 114
Teachings of Buddha, 166
team "snoopervisor," 193
Team Rules, developing your, 151
teamwork, definition of, 40
terrorism, 174
three postures, 120
tough love, 105
trade-offs, opportunity for, 50
traditions, 146-147
Transactional Analysis (TA), 120
transforming opposition into
    innovation, 127, 147, 157, 159, 172,
    175, 180-181, 192-193, 197, 220, 234
tribalism, 173
"try pleasant," 193
turning opposition into innovation,
    107, 116, 134, 151
*29 Questions That Will Energize Your
    Team*, 194
Type A
    introvert, 141
    personalities, 141
tyranny of the *or*, the, 97-98, 108, 178, 227

U

ultimate leader, the, 101
unknown, fearing the, 91
unlimited possibilities, 94
"us versus them," 49

V

Visionary, the, 141, 144, 146, 148-149,
    152, 199-200, 202, 209

W

weird-jerk syndrome, the, 68-69, 145-147
"whackos," the, 68
what goes around comes around, 49
"whole-brained"
    approach, 142, 144
    insight, 143
    thinking, 152
winging it, an element of, 64
win-lose negotiators, 198
"winner take all" mentality, 49
winning through intimidation, 197
Winning Through Intimidation, 46
win-win negotiators, 198

Y

yes/yes principle, the, 136

About the Author
Darby Checketts

Darby grew up on a small ranch in South Phoenix, Arizona. He and Sharon are the parents of seven fantastic children: Natalie, Vance, Denise, Cheryl, Ken, Brent, and Matt. Together with their business partners, Darby and Sharon expound the principles of *Customer Astonishment, Leverage for Leadership in Business and Success in Life*, and now, the timeless principles of *Positive Conflict*. Darby is president of Cornerstone Professional Development, which he founded in 1985. He also serves as its principal consultant and client coach. He has worked with hundreds of organizations, large and small, around the globe. Millions of individuals have benefited from his teachings, his books, and various other publications. His professional career began with Ford Motor Company and includes experience with other fine companies where he served in a variety of management and professional positions. He has traveled throughout the United States and 25 countries on five continents. *Positive Conflict* is Darby's eighth major book. Other recent books are....

Leverage: *How to Create Your Own "Tipping Points" in Business and in Life*

Customer Astonishment: *10 Secrets to World-Class Customer Care*

Please visit *www.DarbyChecketts.com*. Telephone Darby at 866-654-0811. He is available to support you as a coach, strategist, speaker, and all-around resource for education and inspiration.

About *Leverage*

LEVERAGE: How to Create Your Own "Tipping Points" in Business and in Life

By Darby Checketts...with Foreword by best-selling author Steve Chandler

Whatever capabilities you possess to accomplish whatever you've set out to do, you will always benefit from more leverage. Leverage is the multiplier effect that lets you create *tipping points* that help you lift your world. Inspiration for *Leverage* comes from the early Greek mathematician, Archimedes, who once proclaimed, "Give me a lever long enough and a place to stand, and I could lift the world." The book contains 25 keys to greater leverage for leadership in business and success in life. Darby Checketts will show you where your levers are, in every situation. This book is personal. It takes the mystery out of your tipping point opportunities. In the manner of Archimedes, the book will help you ponder and answer two vital questions: Where do you stand? What are your levers? For example, you will....

- o Demystify the idea of *vision* and make it *the* force for getting where you intend to go.
- • Discover what you really *want* and what you must *give* to get it.
- o Embrace the 21st Century standard of excellence: *What is theoretically possible?*
- • Move beyond conflict resolution to harness the *power of opposites.*

- o Turn on your "receptive force" to hear what the world is trying to tell you.
- Make *commitment* the most magnificent word in your vocabulary.
- o Achieve crystal clear agreement with those who share your destiny.
- Discover four distinct dimensions of thinking that will deepen your understanding and invigorate your intuition.
- o Expand your partnerships as the most powerful way to extend your leverage.
- Know the value of what you create to build the wealth that will last.

The book, *Leverage,* is the accumulated wisdom from a life fully lived and from 20 years of interacting with organizations and individuals who are determined to lift their worlds and make a difference. Darby Checketts will take you to memorable places, introduce you to fascinating personalities, and explore situations that illustrate the power of the leverage we all seek.

Leverage Excerpt

Some say this may be *The Age of Fear.* We face such great challenges and yet we have great leverage to help us solve these problems. The heroes of our society may be the engineers and the scientists who are unlocking the keys to faster, sleeker, longer lasting, more affordable everything. Some form of "technology" touches every aspect of our lives, it seems. We hope it holds the answers. We have discovered how to reengineer parts of our bodies. We each carry an encyclopedia of information in our PDAs. Video games simulate everything. Pills change moods, stop pain, cure disease, and stimulate romance. Our worlds vibrate in our purses or pockets as the cell phone "rings"—only it doesn't ring, it plays a symphony or a rapper's punch line.

We seem to be searching for something. We watch reality TV. We hope a popular talk show host will spell it out and reassure us, or a stand-up comic will provide some relief. We look for meaning and purpose. In the end, we usually manage to keep hope alive, juggle the many priorities of our lives, and move on. Still we search.

A little more than a week ago, I sat in the office of a great friend and colleague. Playing in the background was the music of Jeffrey Gaines. I had not heard him before, but I will listen again. The lyrics of his soulful song were punctuated by the line, "There's got to be some hero in me." The words grabbed my attention, uplifted me, distracted me, and continued to haunt me. After all the gadgets have been purchased...after all the pills have been popped...after all the reality TV...after Batman has saved the world....

251

Do I hold the key to me? Are the answers out there somewhere, or in me? Will a UPS truck deliver my happiness, or will I? Can Homeland Security save our nation, or will we? Where's the answer to the problems we see? *There's got to be some hero in me.*

More than 2,000 years ago, the ancient mathematician, Archimedes, spoke these words: *Give me a lever long enough and a place to stand, and I could lift the world.* You are the key to the happiness you seek. The wonders of technology are levers you use, not the answers. You are the most wondrous creation in the universe. You are the answer. This is not the Age of Fear. Archimedes spoke the truth. There is a hero. It's you.

You are a hero as you transform opposition into innovation. Otherwise, the energy inside would be lost. Your communication and negotiation skills are levers that let you harness the power of opposites. As you do, you lift the world.